I meet some friends for drinks and they ask me how the job is going. *Mostly we just stare*, I tell them. They look at me uncertainly. *I love staring*, I say.

JOSHUA JAMES AMBERSON

STARING CONTEST

ESSAYS ABOUT EYES

a Perfect Day book

Several names and identifying characteristics have been changed, and the chronology has occasionally been compressed for clarity.

Staring Contest: Essays about Eyes / Joshua James Amberson
ISBN: 978-1-960200-00-6
Library of Congress Control Number: 2023900080

Advance copies March 2023

Cover design by Aaron Robert Miller
Copyedited by Esa Grigsby
Photo by Yaara Perczek
Perfect Day logo by Corinne Manning
Website by David Small

Printed in the United States of America

www.JoshuaJamesAmberson.com
www.PerfectDayPublishing.com

[PREFACE]

ORIGIN STORIES

A CATALOG

1.

EACH TIME WE HARVESTED THE HONEY there was this: the opening of a secret world, the precision within; the bees in the air, organizing to protect what was rightfully theirs. Most of the year, I didn't think about the junky white boxes on the side of the driveway. But harvesting honey provided a sight so patently different from anything else in my life that for weeks afterward I looked at the boxes with new eyes, temporarily aware of the civilization inside, the elaborate structure of the combs beneath the unremarkable outer surface.

Even more than the microworld of the bees, though, I was transfixed by the beekeeper's suit, its blinding whiteness and thick-screened hood transforming my mom and her boyfriend into creatures, nonhumans. With the single screen and the boxy headpiece, each became a cyclops.

Eventually they let me put on the suit, and I found out that being inside felt less like being a cyclops and more like being a bee. The screen recreated the bees' complex, compound eyes, as if seeing like a bee would assist in breaking into their castle and stealing their labor.

But mostly I liked watching from the sidelines, observing the metamorphosis that happens when a person's face is obscured, when a body becomes a flattened form, a single eye.

2.

Sitting on my grandpa's lap in the living room, I reached up and touched the line, the apparent crack in his bifocals. He turned away, laughing as my untrained fingers came dangerously close to his eyes, smudging his glasses.

"Can you see the crack?" I asked.

"Only if I look for it," he answered, explaining how the prescription was different above the line than it was below. One part of the lens allowed him to see far away, while the other allowed him to see up close.

My attention shifted to my grandma and my uncle, and I noticed the cracks in each of their lenses. My loved ones had multiple visions: two ways of interpreting the world with their glasses on, and a third—a near sightlessness, it seemed—with their glasses off. I looked at the lamp-lit room, the fireplace, the pictures on the mantle, the years-old magazines in the magazine rack, the shelf of home-dubbed VHS tapes, and thought about how it all looked different to me than it did to them.

*

3.

I often think of my mom's refrain: *I've got to put my eyes in.* How I stood behind her as she positioned her face inches from the bathroom mirror, delicately touching her eyeball, letting the plastic lens slide into place, blinking with caution.

I think of the German nurse at my great-grandfather's nursing home who ran her fingernails up my forearm and said, "In my country, we say to never let a caterpillar crawl here or you will go blind," and how I never viewed caterpillars the same again. I think of how I used to stare at the sun dead-on, believing the bright spots that dotted my vision afterward to be proof I had truly experienced something profound. I think of how I regularly took the glasses off the faces of my loved ones and put them onto my own.

And, in all these instances, I swear I see a prescience I probably didn't have. I add up the anecdotes and come to a fascination at the end of the equation: that I was preoccupied with eyes and vision before I needed to be. That, intuitively, I sensed I had a reason to be fascinated. Perhaps I already somehow knew I carried an error inside of me, one that would make me obsess over what we see and how we see, obsess over focus and how to attain it.

4.

In my own mild way, I like to obsess. Or perhaps "obsess" is too strong of a word for what I enjoy. I get interested in a subject, a person, a *something*, and I can't—or at least I don't want to—let it go. A lot of people who become preoccupied like this feel out of control, like the preoccupation has taken over their bodies. And to some degree, I feel that as well. But I also feel a security, a purpose, an equal mix of being chosen by my obsessions and actively choosing them.

This is a book about eyes. Before I started having trouble with my eyes, I never, at least consciously, thought about them. I never thought about how the act of seeing dominated my life and experience of the world. Like most people, I just *saw*.

I started thinking about eyes because I had to. Because there was something wrong with mine. I didn't consider them an interest. It took me years to realize how much time I'd spent—casually, lazily—considering eye-related bits of daily life: the complex social politics of winking, the curious history of eye charts, the emotional impact of overhead lighting. But after I identified the eyes and vision as being interests of mine, I began looking more, looking at things I'd never thought to look at. Now I think about eyes because I want to; it's a preoccupation that feels good to be preoccupied with, even if I wish I'd never been chosen by the subject.

I've come to believe that a single subject has the power to open up the world—that it can serve as an access point to every other subject, that it can make connections that otherwise might not be made. In time, a staring contest became the easiest way for me to think about this: looking long and hard to figure out what's already there. I've never thought of staring contests as combative; to me, they're connective—an agreed-upon chance to be playful while also looking deeply. So I like to imagine I've been staring in an effort to share, to think broadly about the world, to let other people in on a series of questions I don't have answers for.

[ONE]

HAZY

IT STARTS AS A MIST TAKING OVER MY WORLD. For days, I've been cleaning my glasses and dousing my contacts, distracted by a vague fuzziness in my vision. *Make an appointment,* I keep telling myself, *get a new prescription.* But it's all so expensive—the optometrist, the new glasses, the box of contacts. I'm in my mid-twenties, under-employed, uninsured. None of this is in my budget. So I keep cleaning, dousing, trying to overwhelm the haze, trick it into submission.

I'm in a dark movie theater, staring at the bright screen, when I realize the cleaning has been in vain. The images on the screen aren't out of focus; it's more like the film has been manipulated or warped by heat. I close my right eye as a test. To my left eye, an unharmed film plays. Cautiously, I close my left eye, open my right: the characters become distorted shapes, a mess of wandering limbs, torsos melded together into one conjoined body. It seems my left eye is compensating to hide a twisted parallel universe inside my right.

My body stiff, heart pounding, I glance at my friend, wondering if I should tell her. But tell her what? I can't explain it in a sentence I could easily whisper into her ear. And even if I could, would we just leave? It's not as if I can do anything about it at the moment. I've always hated to be an inconvenience, a burden, so I just sit there, rigid. Occasionally, I close my left eye to see if anything has changed—my mind unable to focus on the characters and their petty concerns, unsure of what I am watching.

After the movie, I go to my optometrist, who quickly sends me to an ophthalmologist. The ophthalmologist takes scans, showing me the damage on my retina. Instead of appearing smooth, like a typical retina, the surface of mine resembles cracks in the desert sand, or a topographical map from another planet.

The damage is due to pseudoxanthoma elasticum (PXE), a rare genetic disease I was born with. Though I received the diagnosis as a teenager, I've rarely been forced to think about it. The cracks themselves aren't doing any harm, but they allow for the possibility for blood vessels to penetrate the macula, the retina's most sensitive layer, leaking blood and causing loss of vision. It's not the blood itself that blocks the vision, but the way the blood pushes and stretches the macula, distorting the world.

The doctor tells me I need surgery, and that I have two options. There's a cold laser surgery that has been used for years, he explains, a common procedure, but it doesn't work for most people. Alternatively, there's a drug used in chemotherapy that, as of the past several years, is being used off-label and injected into hemorrhaging eyeballs. It isn't a surgery, but rather an injection they approach with the caution of a surgery. So far, it's had a very high success rate, and the risk, he assures me, is worth it.

I'm broke—my job at an adored but perpetually struggling independent bookstore pays barely more than minimum wage—so I tell him I'll need a couple months to get funding together. He shakes his head, clearly frustrated that I'm not getting it. He says I can't wait, that the process is rapid, and if I don't get treated within the coming weeks, I will be blind in that eye.

Irreversible, he keeps saying. *If you wait, the blindness will be irreversible.*

Early in my childhood, I realized I could alter the world around me anytime I wanted. Simply by squinting, crossing my eyes, and fluttering my eyelashes, I could induce an entirely different experience of reality. It was as if I could turn on an inner strobe light, creating partial images, moments between moments.

Lying in bed, I transformed the hazy morning light coming through the blinds—already diffused by a layer of Northwest clouds—into a spiritual experience. I imagined the flickering, soft light was what the afterlife looked like, what God looked like. I felt the out-of-focus was closer to the divine.

Of course, I wasn't alone in this. Most artistic and cinematic representations of heavenly things took place in the haze of clouds. In some divine representations, subjects were so bathed in clouds and sun they became more illumination than image. And it wasn't limited to religion. Most alternate realms and beings were presented as hazy—dreams and ghosts, other dimensions, the act of time travel. I had taken the popular representations as fact, and, in the morning light, I felt sure I was accessing one of these realms, tuning in to something below the surface, hidden.

I could only blur my eyes for short stretches since the act was mildly painful. One time, I tried to test my endurance, keeping the fluttering going for minutes, and came out of it with a soreness that lingered for the rest of the day. I worried I had damaged my eyes permanently.

But once the soreness passed, I used the pain as proof of the activity's importance: I imagined I was engaged in the work of visionaries and artists, those who suffered for the sake of experience and did something with those hard-earned experiences. But I wasn't doing anything other than experiencing, and, as an endlessly concerned child, I sometimes wondered where all this practice would lead. Most days, though, it was enough to rediscover that the world was not static, but malleable.

Blurring was an option anytime I wanted to change reality. Life forced us into so much—there was my mom with the two jobs she hated, my grandma with her graveyard shifts at the hospital, the daily awkwardness of elementary school. Everyone I knew was doing something they didn't want to do. But life also offered ways to escape, to transcend.

Doctors compare retinal hemorrhaging to taking a projector screen and bending it. The world is still visible, but curved, its details lost within the arcs. When my alarm goes off the morning after my appointment, I open my eyes, and—even without my glasses—know immediately that the screen has bent a little further. After putting on my glasses, I notice how the light fixtures droop, how the art on the walls merges, how everything lacks detail. I walk to my job at the bookstore, my left eye working hard to compensate, trying to adjust to this new vision. It takes hours for it to not be jarring. Then, when the sun goes down, I have to adjust again.

Walking home that night, the streetlights blur together. Businesses and apartment buildings lose their doors and windows and signs, morphing into single distorted balls of illumination. When I look away, the whole world twinkles in my periphery, as if it's all decorated for the holidays, horrifying and beautiful. I've never been so aware of light, how qualities of light can so dramatically change the experience of reality. The next morning I wake up, my vision altered, and begin the process all over again.

I never told my mom about how often I blurred my eyes, because I knew she would claim it wasn't good for me. More than that, though, these experiences felt private—acts that might lose their magic if I talked about them.

But since I loved the blur so much, I created a performative version that I enacted at stoplights while my mom drove us around. Leaning forward in my seat, blurring my eyes, and speaking in my best imitation of a hypnotist, I chanted, "Melt in my eyes, turn green," elongating the vowels with each recitation until the light changed.

I liked how it made my mom laugh, how—if I wasn't

paying attention and a light was taking a particularly long time—she requested it.

Hey Josh, can you help with this light?

The truth is, I took the responsibility seriously. I believed that if I focused my energy and unfocused my eyes enough, I could do it. I just had to tense the muscles in my body and put their strength to work toward one goal: my gaze intensifying, the illuminated red sinking into the un-illuminated yellow and green, losing its hold over us. Sometimes I believed I could feel the blur working.

Finding a doctor who gives the injections isn't easy. I live in Olympia, the capital of Washington State, and there isn't a single clinic in the city or its suburbs that can help me. The nearest clinic that offers the injections is located thirty miles south at a cataract and laser institute in Chehalis. Though they don't have a full-time surgeon who performs the procedure, once a week a surgeon comes and injects eyeballs all day long. He does this all across western Washington, each day at a different clinic in a different city.

Because of their relative scarcity, each shot costs over a thousand dollars, and a series of shots are required. Hemorrhaging often recurs, so the first series is sometimes just the beginning. With no idea how I will pay for it, I schedule an appointment.

I consider myself independent, a bit of a loner, secretly too proud for any kind of assistance, so I usually try to avoid asking for help. But I've also been raised in a lower-middle class family who taught me that debt is a type of personal failure. Aside from going blind, debt is my greatest fear, and

I've nearly made it through the first decade of my adult life free of it. So I am either going to owe money for the rest of my life, or I am going to ask for help.

After some searching and soliciting recommendations from friends, I find a healthcare advocate: an eccentric man with glaucoma who is passionate about hunting, electric guitars, and obtaining healthcare for low-income people. He's part of an advocacy group whose office is tucked away in a strip mall next to a cemetery. In the back of the office, past a mess of movable walls and stacked boxes, he has a cubicle.

Day after day, he walks me through medical assistance forms. We hold conference calls with social service organizations and email church groups. We even call the Knights of Columbus, a Masons-like group of Catholic men that he knows fund eye surgeries because he once tried to become a Knight. We end up making an appointment with the Knights' treasurer at his home, the first trailer at the only trailer park in the backwoods town of Elma.

My age catches everyone off guard. Typically, only the elderly receive retinal treatments, and every assistance program is designed with this in mind. No one can figure out what to do with an apparently healthy boyish twentysomething, whose eyes show no hints of their internal issues.

More rejection letters come. The idea is that we can take all these letters and turn them over to somebody, some organization, somewhere, and it will mean something. After every medical assistance organization we've applied to turns down our applications, my advocate and I fax each of the rejection letters to the laser clinic in Chehalis.

Then we wait.

I've still heard nothing the day before the first injection is scheduled, so I assume I'll have to postpone. I fill out credit card applications, imagining having to suck up my pride and borrow money from friends and family. I wonder how waiting another week will affect my eye.

Then, late in the day, I get a letter saying the clinic will cover the treatments through their emergency assistance program. I celebrate, briefly relieved, before realizing that the coverage suddenly makes the injections real. Now I can't put them off.

Knowing I need to steel myself, I spend the night watching the only film I can think of with a moment of eye harm: *Un Chien Andalou*, a 1929 surrealist short film by Luis Buñuel and Salvador Dalí. The film's most memorable element, and the scene that's become a staple for disturbing film collages, is the moment where a doctor slices a woman's eyeball in half.

Between viewings, I read everything I can about PXE, joining its D.C.-based international nonprofit advocacy group. I research the seemingly endless list of side effects for the drug that is going to get shot into my eye. I watch the film one last time before going to bed. When the doctor cuts the eyeball, I don't flinch.

In third grade, a craze began around a book called *Magic Eye*. I didn't understand the attraction. It was filled with pages of ugly, pixelated patterns that supposedly held some secret I couldn't access. Other kids told me to just blur my eyes, and, each time they said it, a sadness washed over me.

Things like this always happened to me as a shy only child: I thought I was good at something, thought I knew a subject so well, then found out my abilities or knowledge hadn't been challenged or pushed by outside forces. My ability to blur the world—to access other realms—was obviously lacking. There were dinosaurs and planets behind those walls of patterned nonsense, and I couldn't blur my eyes enough to see them.

Magic Eye went from being a single book, an annoying oddity, to an entire franchise. Notebooks, bookmarks, binders, glossy posters. And with each item, I felt more and more certain that a spiritual practice was being sold and exploited. Blurring the eyes was supposed to be something sublime, something that could change the world around you. But here it was cheapened, apparently revealing unremarkable boats and statues, things you could see anytime.

The morning of my first injection—even though I've prepared, even though it's funded—I still hold on to the possibility that there might be another way. Until now, the sole doctor I've seen only knows about these treatments from medical journals. I haven't been to this clinic, haven't met this doctor. I go in, hoping this new doctor will respond to the questions I have about the drug and together we can weigh the risks.

But as soon as he enters the room, a team of nurses slips in behind him. Gloves are being put on, little metal tables are being filled with tools, and I can't seem to stop the forward motion.

Finally, I raise my voice enough to ask about what I've read: the treatment's newness, its unknowns, its potential side effects. The doctor stares at me, clearly uninterested in the questions.

He remains quiet several beats longer than is comfortable. "Yes, those side effects are certainly possible," he finally says.

"You could experience headaches or nosebleeds, you could have hair loss, everyone reacts differently. We could insert this into your eye, you could be allergic, and you could go blind instantly. Or we could do nothing, and you'd be blind in a month. Those are our options."

My body tightens, the emotionless weight of his logic sinking in. In some not-so-distant part of my brain, I've known this was the answer all along, but I'd wanted to be coddled into acknowledging it. I consider the emergency funding, expressions of gratitude versus the scale of my anxiety, the simultaneous bets we are placing, and, finally, I nod.

With my right eye clamped open, the nurses and the doctor hovering over me, and my roommate, who has casually given me a ride, nervously watching from the corner of the room, I realize I haven't asked a very essential question. "How do I not watch the needle go in?"

The doctor answers, "Look up and to the left."

I do and immediately feel as if I've been toppled by a wave and pulled under. A rush of bright, cloudy fluid enters my vision and spreads, crossing from my right eye over to my left, moving in all directions at once.

Unable to see out of either eye, I assume I'm one of those rare allergic cases. Everything is white and thick, blurred and bright. But soon the shapes of the hovering nurses reappear, the fluid slowly clears. And in the wake of that brief, profound experience of horror and undeniable beauty, I feel momentarily ecstatic, unconcerned about the drug in my eyeball or what it means for the future.

*

The injections happen in a series of three, one a month. Within a few days of my first injection, my vision begins to clear up. Soon after my second injection, I stop noticing any distortion. The third just feels like overkill.

In a way, I'm thankful for the excess, because it seems like it seals the deal. We've gone above and beyond, and because of that, I become convinced that my eye will be better far into the future. But less than a year later, I have another hemorrhage. Hemorrhaging in the same eye, another series of shots.

Not long after that, at the beginning of a two-month tour with a band I'm playing in, I grow convinced that my eye is hemorrhaging again. Behind the wheel, looking through the windshield into sunny California, it seems obvious. The distortion is too peculiar to be normal.

I decide to call my clinic, thinking I might have to quit the tour and catch a bus home so that I can get the financially covered treatments. My insides tighten and curl into a private, internal fit. It seems so unfair to me that everyone I know can take a trip without worrying like this, and now I am going to have to be forever protective, on guard.

But when I call, they tell me their one location outside the Northwest is in Albuquerque, New Mexico, and that if I go there, they will honor the emergency funding. We're playing a show in Albuquerque in a week, so I make an appointment.

This turn of events is absolutely a relief, a cause for celebration, but the appointment also has the effect of turning me into an inconvenience, the kind of burden I try to avoid being. Our tour has us playing in a different city or town every night and now we have to squeeze one more thing into this tight schedule, going out of our way, because of me. On the way to Albuquerque, we hit traffic, then get lost on the way to the clinic, and find ourselves running down its expansive halls, trying to locate the office for my appointment.

This isn't anything like the humble single-floored clinic I go to in Washington, but rather a multi-level facility that seems to cater to an entirely different class of people. In our cutoff shorts and thin T-shirts, out of breath, road worn—my curls untamed in the unfamiliar heat, my female tourmates' legs and armpits characteristically unshaven—to onlookers, we probably look like we've arrived from another planet.

I get all the tests and I was wrong. There is no hemorrhage, nothing to treat. Instead, I learn that I have developed permanent damage from the hemorrhaging—scar tissue, essentially—and I've mistaken that uncorrectable distortion for new bleeding. The dramatic change from gray Northwest skies to the perpetual sun of California and the Southwest means that I can see the damage more clearly; it was the light that fooled me.

Embarrassed about having made such a fuss over nothing, I ask if there is a way I can test myself in the future. They hand me a piece of paper. It's a four-by-five-inch sheet, poorly xeroxed, with a simple grid of uniform squares.

I don't know exactly what I expected, but I want more than this. At the very least I want several pieces of paper, a series of exercises to practice—some new way of viewing the world. But they tell me that this, a grid developed in the 1940s, is the only at-home option. If the eye is hemorrhaging, the grid's lines become wavy, like the boxes are a net, blowing in the wind.

Back on the road, I try using the grid, but it feels as futile as staring at a *Magic Eye* image—there is nothing there, nothing to gain from it or understand, even though I've been assured that there is. I focus my attention on it, wishing I could just see the blood so I'd know.

But with the permanent damage, the lines are always a little wavy. And each time I look, the lines seem slightly different. If I stare with the assumption that I might be experiencing the beginning of a hemorrhage—a "leak," as they call it—then the lines look wavier. If I stare at it thinking I am just experiencing the effects of the damage, the lines appear to be less wavy.

So I invent my own tests as I go about my days. Close my left eye and look at a street sign. The page of a book. A billboard in the distance. A computer screen. The graffiti on a lamppost. From this I try to determine if what I am seeing is permanent damage or a new hemorrhage. Sometimes it works and it's clear what is what. But there are so many variables, so much to consider—the weather, the time of day, whether a room is lit overhead or by lamp—each of these factors changes the quality of light, and light is vision. On top of that, my emotional state, my stress level, and how much I've slept also affect my sight. The more I pay attention, the less sure I am.

I no longer need to blur my eyes to see things differently. I just close my left eye and a new world opens up. It's not an escape, nor transcendent, not like the blur I experienced as a kid. It's distorted, rough, and sometimes it shakes me, fills me with loss—even though the actual loss is so small, a tiny hint of what it could be.

I've always assumed that the difference between permanent and new would eventually become obvious. But if anything, I've just become more paranoid as the years have gone by, more preoccupied with details. I call my right eye "my one bad eye." While my left eye compensates most of the time, I've begun to notice the damage in certain ways light is transmitted. Bright sun through a window, overhead lighting in an office building, a thin layer of clouds reflected in water.

At least a few times each year, the light makes me question what I'm seeing, and I can't let it go. I keep focusing on the damage, and, in this focusing, I stop being able to differentiate. I call my eye doctor, schedule an emergency appointment, only to be wrong again.

The doctors call it "scar creep"; the damage from the hemorrhages is expanding on its own, altering my vision for the worse along the way. My vision is never static. It's always shifting.

The damage is clearest when I look at the moon. I've been a night owl my whole life, and the moon always fills me with a rush of energy, a particular awareness of being alive I don't have during the day. I'm more myself when the moon comes out. I teach night classes, and often, when I walk home and turn the corner onto my quiet block, the moon hangs low in the sky, illuminating my path. But as my vision changes, the moon grows fuzzier, a ball of light shifting in and out of focus. To look at it makes me woozy, unsteady on my feet.

But to look at it also feels important, necessary—an opening to the blurred alternate realm that's a part of me, and also more than me.

[TWO]

THE EYE PATCH

A BRIEF HISTORY

WHEN I WAS ELEVEN, the new jack swing group TLC burst onto the stage of whatever live TV show was playing in our living room. Down went the baseball cards that I'd been organizing; I watched the performance, rapt. The members of TLC wore giant colorful overalls and oversized hats, with Lisa "Left Eye" Lopes standing center stage, sporting a condom eye patch. I would later learn that Left Eye didn't wear the eye patch for any functional purpose—it was just part of the group's safe-sex-endorsing, condom-strewn wardrobe. It wasn't even a patch in the traditional sense, just a condom set into a pair of costume glasses, but I didn't know that at the time. As a white kid without older siblings in the rural Pacific Northwest, I didn't know what TLC's condom clothes meant, didn't understand why said clothes didn't fit them, and certainly didn't realize that the chorus of "Ain't 2 Proud 2 Beg" was a joyful celebration of penises of all lengths and degrees of firmness, but I loved the whole spectacle. Especially the patch.

My first exposure to the eye patch was likely on fictional pirates. The eye patch is their most recognizable signifier; the simplest pirate Halloween costume you can buy is a paper mask with an eye patch drawn onto it. When you wear it, everyone knows what your costume is. But this image, like many things I believed in my childhood, is not true. Or at least it isn't widely true.

There doesn't seem to be any well-known pirate from the Golden Age of Piracy or beyond that can be proven to have worn an eye patch. The patched pirate appears to be an invention born in fictional representation, but the origins of this invention are muddy. Though sailors were often caricatured with eye patches, there are no patch-sporting pirates in any of the influential eighteenth- and nineteenth-century sources for our modern image—*A General History of the Pyrates*, *Treasure Island*, *Peter Pan*, *The Pirates of Penzance*—or in the surviving theatrical descriptions of pirate costumes from the nineteenth and early twentieth centuries. One theory is that it was the patched Long John Silver from the now-lost 1920 silent-film adaptation of *Treasure Island* that placed the patch into the popular imagination. An *Our Gang* short featured a prominent pirate patch a few years later, and by the time Disney picked up on the image for a Mickey Mouse short a decade later, there was an entire pirate crew with patches. The image had spread. Some who don't want to believe that the patch is an invention suggest real pirates used eye patches not to protect an empty socket from infection, but to keep one eye adjusted to night vision for going below deck—a technique the United States Navy employed during World War II—but this is just a fun possibility rather than a historical fact.

Growing up, I mostly knew eye patches from movies. It often meant tough: John Wayne in *True Grit*, Kurt Russell in *Escape from New York*, Adolfo Celi as the suave Bond villain in *Thunderball*. But it also sometimes meant silly: Steve Martin in *Dirty Rotten Scoundrels*, or Chevy Chase in *Spies Like Us*. Sometimes these meanings combined into a cartoonish cool that often existed off-screen: Sammy Davis Jr. before he got his glass eye; David Bowie as alter ego Ziggy Stardust; famed Northwest glass artist Dale Chihuly, who was a staple of Seattle public television throughout my childhood; or actual cartoon character Bazooka Joe, whose gum-paired comic strips I collected.

But soon after seeing TLC, my associations with the eye patch largely became connected to hip-hop. As with many other hip-hop histories, the story here begins with Slick Rick, the genre's most sampled artist. In South London, as an infant, his right eye was blinded by a shard of glass from a broken window. He began wearing the eye patch when coming up as a rapper in the Bronx in the mid-eighties to stick out in the crowd. This soon evolved into his full-blown image as The Ruler, or the "Black Liberace," covering himself in rings and chains, the king of cartoon-cool. I mainly encountered Slick Rick in record store bargain bins, his covers looking like skewed after-school specials. Unaware of his renown, to me he was just the eye patch guy who did "La Di Da Di" and had albums no one seemed to want any more.

When I was eighteen, I bought De La Soul's *Buhloone Mindstate* at Goodwill. Putting it on the moment I got home, I was immediately swept up in the off-kilter groove of the opening track, "Eye Patch." The seemingly nonsensical lyrics ("Can the cat's tongue slip, you do the da zip / Take the horse into the jolly ranch / Keep the hush") were, to me, wide-open for interpretation and provided no clues about the eye patch of the song's title. So, I relied on the song's opening refrain—more incantation than chorus—for meaning: "Mess up my mind, mess up my mind, mess up my mind with the eye patch."

At the time, I assumed it was a song about a girl with an eye patch and interpreted it as a celebration of unconventional beauty—akin to a love of crooked teeth, of facial scars, or unusually placed moles. I first heard the song in 2000, seven years after it came out, a year when "Back That Azz Up," "Thong Song," and "Whistle While You Twurk" dominated pop radio. While all fine songs in their own right, they were songs that paid tribute to oft-celebrated aspects of female beauty. But I'd never heard anyone celebrate an eye patch. What a wonderful thing, I thought. Later, I learned the song was actually a takedown of record label executives who were trying to make De La's clever, playful take on hip-hop more accessible to the masses by attempting to cover the group's metaphorical third eye with a patch.

Since then, the eye patch has become regularly celebrated on-screen as an accoutrement of unconventional female beauty and strength. The origins of tough women with eye patches in film and TV can probably be traced to Bette Davis as the controlling matriarch in *The Anniversary*, but it's Wendy Robie as the superhumanly strong Nadine on *Twin Peaks* who defined the trope and created a legacy that continued on *Pushing Daisies* and *Doctor Who*. On the other hand, the sexualization of eye-patched female strength may have originated in nineties anime, or perhaps the late-nineties rise in steampunk fashion, and was popularized by Daryl Hannah in Quentin Tarantino's 2003 film *Kill Bill*. This was followed by sexy eye patches in *Sky Captain and the World of Tomorrow*, *The Mindy Project*, *Pride and Prejudice and Zombies*, *The Favourite*, and *Chicana Stardust*. Not to mention contemporary anime, where eye-patched female characters with giant breasts in tight clothes are abundant—from my outside perspective, an apparently full-blown fetish—and are present in at least a dozen series in recent years.

Because of this prevalence, eye patches are perceived by most people to be more of a film trope than a thing people actually wear. Instead of being a real-world tool, it's a Hollywood shorthand that, according to writer Hanh Nguyen, signifies "some sort of trauma" and shows "a badge of suffering." Nguyen observes that an eye patch can also be a way to set a character apart by giving them "a dangerous, rakish or even quirky air." And this shorthand has never been more common.

We are arguably in the heyday of eye patches on-screen. In addition to the recent eye-patched women, patched men have appeared in *Buffy the Vampire Slayer*, *Harry Potter*, *Battlestar Galactica*, *The Invention of Hugo Cabret*, *Lost*, *Mad Men*, *A Series of Unfortunate Events*, *Game of Thrones*, *Oz*, *The Walking Dead*, *The Avengers*, and of course the *Pirates of the Caribbean* movies.

I always enjoy seeing an eye patch on-screen. Even at its toughest, it's always a little cartoonish, always over-the-top—something theatrical and fun. But when I sit in ophthalmologists' waiting rooms, the people wearing eye patches are just regular people with appointments. They're often construction workers in their safety vests, likely experiencing an eye injury. Or they're elderly people, often in wheelchairs, who, given what I know about the average older person in the waiting rooms I frequent, have most likely lost sight in an eye due to diabetes-related complications. They're definitely never over-the-top cartoons. They're never visibly tough or silly or cool. They're just stuck with an unwanted practical tool that most people think of as a playful costume accessory.

Rarely, if ever, does the actor behind an eye-patched character use one off-screen. Wearing an eye patch eliminates binocular vision—the result of both eyes working together, allowing people to create three-dimensional images and judge distance—which affects depth perception and peripheral vision, but eye-patched characters are often more agile than their two-eyed opponents. In terms of film tropes, this makes it a close cousin of the "blind seer," where a visual limitation leads not only to more finely tuned non-ocular senses, but great wisdom and near-magical abilities.

Off the screen and outside of waiting rooms, the eye patch is a rare sight. "I'm usually the only person walking down the street with a patch on," Slick Rick says. Kids with eye patches—who often wear them to strengthen an amblyopic (or "lazy") eye—frequently get bullied. From what I've read, they usually don't turn into raffish antiheroes who fight back, or become the stars of the school talent show, but instead suffer from low self-esteem.

Rick believes that having one eye determined who he became. Instead of playing in the streets with the other kids, "I stayed indoors and wrote stories," he says. The dozen times I've had a retinal hemorrhage, I've wondered who I would become if I lost vision in the hemorrhaging eye and donned a patch. It's usually just a silly question of aesthetics more than a real worry—a distraction for my mind—but it happens every time. Any hints of cool left my style as soon as I turned thirty, and I currently feel most comfortable in the sweaters and vintage button-ups worn by straitlaced dads of past eras, so an eye patch would be a surprising addition to my wardrobe. I would, very suddenly, present differently to the world.

One day, I decide to buy an eye patch from the drugstore. While I've had very little sight out of one eye many times, I've never had either eye completely covered for longer than it takes to read some letters from an eye chart.

The patch is black with a strap, like I'd hoped it would be, but it's also padded, which I hadn't anticipated. When I put the patch on in the parking lot behind the store, the padding makes it so that my glasses barely fit back on my face. They sit precariously on the end of my nose, a little crooked. The patch is also giant—nearly twice the size of what I'd expected. Catching my reflection in a car window, I can see that I am, objectively, a mess. I left the house early this morning, without a shower, having covered myself in a random assortment of layers and a haphazardly tied scarf. Due to a side effect from a medication I've been taking, I've been losing hair rapidly in recent months, turning what's left of my already unruly hair into something even more gravity defying, and its state at the moment is absurdly windblown. I don't look cool, but I'm certainly a cartoon.

I feel my brain retraining itself, furiously adjusting to the new limitations of the patch. Without binocular vision or much peripheral vision, I have to turn my head fully to each side before crossing the street, rather than employing the slight glances I can normally get away with, but that's the only immediate challenge. I walk through my neighborhood, past the pizza joint, the coffee shop, the sandwich place where the uniformly pretty people eat Midwestern food. Other than my favorite barista doing a double take through the window, no one seems to pay me much mind. When I get home, my roommates aren't there, so there's no one to surprise with my new, temporary addition. I walk to the bathroom, remove the patch in front of the mirror, taking note of how its absence turns my face back into something more recognizable, and as light floods my senses, my eyes excitedly join forces once again. I make myself a cup of tea and pull up an early TLC live performance on my phone, swiftly forgetting my experiment, my toe-dip into the land of what-ifs, and I return to a place where an eye patch is just a matter of aesthetics, a playful accessory, a Halloween costume, something actors wear.

[THREE]

CORRECTIVE

IN FOURTH GRADE, MY AGING TEACHER'S neat handwriting began to morph into a series of arcane, jumbled symbols, their formerly straight lines and perfect circles turning wavy and uneven. I wondered if Mr. Youngren was getting shaky as time went by, or if it was an issue with the chalk, or even the board itself. My confusion continued for weeks, maybe even months.

Then one day, as I squinted, struggling to read the fuzzy brand of chalk our school insisted on buying, an obvious explanation occurred to me: I needed glasses. Throughout my family—across my dozens of cousins, my aunts and uncles, my grandparents and great-grandparents—everyone except me and my two younger cousins had a pair. Before now, I hadn't considered what this meant for me, or perhaps I hadn't allowed myself to consider it, but once I realized what was happening, it became evident that I had been doomed to wear glasses all along. Yet, even when the inevitable arrived, I wasn't ready to accept it.

This took place during an era when the makeover movie thrived. Through a simple style change, the status of a film's character could suddenly be elevated, their rise meteoric. Almost always, this included the character ditching their glasses, thereby showing the world that they were not the unattractive loser everyone thought they were. With this simple deletion, girls went from gross to model-pretty and boys transformed from nerds into suave womanizers. Though my shy disposition and bargain-store clothing made me strikingly similar to the losers in the first acts of the makeover movies, my idols were baseball and basketball players—muscular men who were quick to anger and uniformly unencumbered by optical lenses. I watched Ami Dolenz in *She's Out of Control*, Patrick Dempsey in *Can't Buy Me Love*, and the message was simple: glasses not only symbolized ugliness, but also weakness.

Glasses historian Neil Handley notes that, "In many languages other than English, they're often described as a prosthesis; an artificial part of the body, part of you, making you who you are." In the United States, through at least the 1930s, eyeglasses were classified as "medical appliances" and were largely stigmatized as a visible sign of disability through the first half of the twentieth century. A study that came out in the *Journal of Social Psychology* around the time I was born found that participants judged a male model wearing glasses to be "weaker and more of a follower than participants who viewed the same male model without eyeglasses." While glasses typically solved a vision issue, making the wearer more capable, they also announced a lack, an underlying structural error.

My deepest fear was that I would reveal this error in myself, this inner weakness. Glasses were social death for fourth graders in the early nineties in rural Washington. There were only two or three kids in each class with glasses, and these kids always held a low social standing. I was already a chubby, awkward only child who lived in a trailer in the woods and was sometimes dropped off at school in a rusty mail delivery jeep. Thus far, despite all the possible jokes that could be made at my expense, I'd largely learned to slip under the bully radar.

I had switched schools when the district rezoned after second grade, but my first few years were at a school deep in the country, populated by the children of farmers and rural recluses—years that had left a deep impression on me. The toys on our playground included large cement pipes made for sewer systems and wood pallets attached to springs. Fights broke out every recess, and kids got picked on for a variety of seemingly insignificant reasons—preppy clothes, nasally voices, odd gaits—but glasses were by far the most common cause. They were right there, perched on one's nose, sticking out. You couldn't miss them.

Before the arrival of corrective lenses, both farsighted and nearsighted people lived with a disability. While farsighted people struggled with reading and close work, nearsighted people made their way through a world without details—hazy shapes, blocks of color, streaks of movement. No one knows for sure when eyeglasses were invented, but the best guess is thirteenth-century Italy. The concept of looking through glass, crystal, or globes of water to assist with vision had been around since ancient times, but the glasses that became popular in Italy were the first we know of that were held to the eyes rather than the page.

These glasses were reading glasses, solely addressing far-sightedness, and it wasn't until the sixteenth century that glasses attempted to address nearsightedness. I often think about that wait—centuries passing, generations of families hoping for a tool to make their lives less difficult. What did it feel like to witness so many having their vision improved while your far more debilitating issue went wholly ignored? Even after the development of lenses for nearsightedness, glasses were still largely understood—perhaps because of the social conventions established by reading glasses—to be a practical tool to be used only occasionally. "Wearing spectacles or eyeglasses out of doors is always a disfigurement, often an injury, seldom a necessity," an early twentieth-century article in *New York Medical Journal* stated.

Nearly a century later, as a ten-year-old, I carried on this tradition of considering glasses a disfigurement. It didn't matter that most of the adults I knew and loved wore glasses because in my mind glasses were just one of the many possible embarrassing liabilities that came with adulthood. Glasses on kids were simply different. My new school wasn't as rough as my previous one, but I held on to the sense of caution I'd developed as a younger child. I was careful not to say anything that could be used against me, careful not to get too carried away when playing games and risk showing an unflattering side of myself, careful not to advertise that I was being careful. Every Monday, the symbols on the board looked a little fuzzier than the week before, but I was resourceful. I became adept at writing quickly, capturing Mr. Youngren's words as they left his mouth. When I lost track, or when he wrote on the board without speaking at the same time, I copied notes from my neighbors. Months went by with no one the wiser.

Then one day Mr. Youngren asked me to read the quote he'd written on the board for the class. I balked, trying to pass off the responsibility to one of my classmates. When that didn't work, I squinted, reading the words I could make out. "Should . . . that . . . and . . . to," I said, conscious of how much the moment resembled this one particular *ABC Afterschool Special* I'd seen a half-dozen times where a kid who can't read is exposed in front of everyone. My classmates chuckled, my face and neck turned red, and Mr. Youngren, well aware of my reading abilities, said, "Would you like to move closer to the board?"

I didn't want to, but nevertheless I nodded, admitting defeat. I moved to the front of the room, read the quote, and soon found myself in a meeting with Mr. Youngren and my mom, discussing my need for glasses. All the questions I'd worked so hard to never hear flowed freely. How long had it been going on? Why didn't I tell anyone? Was I being picked on by other kids? I mumbled a string of *no*s and *I don't know*s, trying to convince time to move faster, to escape the interrogation room and get back to blending in.

On the ride home, my mom casually suggested that I give contacts a try. Not knowing anyone my age who wore contacts, I hadn't considered them a possibility before, but immediately celebrated the idea and assumed my problem was solved. However, when I went to my eye appointment, the elderly optometrist told me that kids couldn't properly deal with contacts until they were teenagers. I was a tidy kid who organized my room for fun; my mom and I both knew I could handle contacts. But to the optometrist, I was just another child who couldn't be trusted with tiny, delicate pieces of plastic. When he told me that I'd have to wait another three years to get contacts—an eternity in my mind—I looked to my mom with desperation, silently begging her to save me from this man and his foolish, antiquated ideas. But I'd inherited my fear of conflict from her, and she just shrugged her shoulders, giving me her apologetic look of defeat.

It seems likely that as soon as eyeglasses came into existence, there were inventors and glasses wearers dreaming of how to trade them in for something less cumbersome and obvious. The long and painful history of contact lenses can be traced back to 1508 when Leonardo da Vinci created, as a way to potentially improve vision, a glass lens into which water could be funneled. In 1636, working off da Vinci's idea, philosopher René Descartes proposed placing a similar glass tube on the cornea itself. But it wasn't until 1801 that an English scientist named Thomas Young actually put the idea to use, making a basic pair of contact lenses that he glued to his own eyeballs with wax.

However, these early water-filled contacts barely addressed most vision issues, and it wasn't until 1845 that English astronomer Sir John Herschel suggested taking a mold of the cornea and then applying "transparent animal jelly contained in a spherical capsule of glass," in the shape of that mold, to the eye. In the 1880s, German ophthalmologist Adolf Fick, using similar principles but apparently unaware of Herschel's idea, wrote the treatise "A Contact Spectacle," laying out how contacts could be used for visual improvement—information he acquired through experiments he'd conducted on the eyes of rabbits, his own eyes, and those of a small, brave group of volunteers.

Having been denied contacts, I went to school the next week with a clunky pair of glasses in my backpack. As I worked up the courage to put them on, I noticed that my teacher didn't seem to care that I wasn't wearing them. I soon understood that I was only expected to wear them in one situation: when taking notes off the board. So I just left them tucked away in my desk drawer and, when the time came, quietly slipped them out of their case, dipped my head as if checking for a lost eraser, and put them on.

But by middle school, this selective use became an issue. My vision had gotten bad enough that I couldn't see further than a few feet in front of me. One day, I saw a human shape waving from down the hall. I peeked behind me and didn't see anyone waving back, but decided waving was too risky. What if it was someone popular who had never acknowledged me, waving to someone else who had even less interest in my existence? The fallout could be catastrophic. So, I put my head down and ignored the still-waving hand. Then a pair of doodled-on Converse All Stars appeared on the floor in front of me, and I looked up at the angry face of my best friend Stephanie.

I tried explaining I hadn't seen her.

"You looked right at me," she said. "Then you looked away. That sent a pretty clear message."

A few months later I went in for my annual eye exam. Even though I was still just twelve years old, the optometrist wrote me a contact prescription as if my age had never been an issue. While watching him write it, I thought about everything I had endured, and how the solution was as simple as a few numbers and a signature on a small, unremarkable piece of paper.

The first person to create a working example of the contact lenses Adolf Fick proposed was glass-eye maker F. A. Mueller in 1887. Mueller's contacts were made of heavy blown glass, and they covered the entire exposed eyeball, rather than just the cornea. This proved to be a significant flaw; unlike the rest of the body, which the blood oxygenates, the eye receives its oxygen from the air. Consequently, these impermeable lenses cut off the oxygen supply completely, and just a few hours of use produced acute eye pain. Despite their drawbacks, these were the most common contacts until the 1920s. The invention of new plastics bumped Mueller's invention from the top spot, but it wasn't until the 1960s that contacts began letting oxygen into the eye, and not until the late 1990s—several years after I got my first pair—that contacts with high-oxygen permeability became widely available.

I'd scarcely had a chance to celebrate my contacts, or bemoan the pain they caused me, before my mom took an interest in what she perceived to be a new ailment of mine: the way my neck was dotted with small lumps, similar to gooseflesh, as if it was permanently cold. Given how self-conscious I was about my appearance, I'd oddly thought nothing of it; my acne and seemingly impossible-to-control curly hair took up the bulk of my concerns. But my mom worried I was having an allergic reaction, so she dragged me to our small-town family practitioner.

What we'd both expected to be a straightforward appointment soon turned strange. Instead of telling us to change the laundry detergent we used, or to get rid of shirts made of synthetic materials, the doctor examined my inner elbows in addition to my neck and asked questions about my vision, his brow furrowed. Then he walked off, disappearing for longer than seemed reasonable, before returning with a bulky medical textbook. He showed us a page, deep in the back of the book, which displayed photographs of an armpit, the inside of an eyeball, and a neck that looked just like mine. He explained that the goosebumps were actually called papules, and papules on the neck were a telltale early sign of a rare condition called pseudoxanthoma elasticum, or PXE, that affects the elasticity of tissue. "It's something I read about in medical school," he said, "but never thought I'd see."

PXE presents visible symptoms at the soft places where the body bends: the neck, the inside of the knee and the elbow, the groin, the armpit. The doctor pointed out how, on each of these places on my body, the skin was slightly wrinkled, adorned with tiny papules. None were as pronounced as the ones on my neck, but they were there. Having always assumed that this was just what bodies looked like, I studied these spots with horror, wondering what other parts of me were secret, freakish signs of an inner fragility.

Though not much was known about the condition, in some cases patients experienced the progressive degeneration of their internal organs. Some suffered from gastrointestinal bleeding and blood clots. And everyone with the condition developed cracks on the retina called angioid streaks. The family practitioner sent us to Seattle Children's Hospital, but doctors there knew little more than he did. "You'll either never be affected by it," one of the doctors told me, "or someday you'll go blind."

One might assume that the threat of blindness changed something in me—delivering some new appreciation for life or snapping me out of the frivolous drama of whether to wear glasses or not—but it didn't. The condition was just a fact, something that was for the moment held inside my body, largely invisible. Glasses weren't. So I put the condition as far out of my mind as I could and kept wearing contacts, even though they weren't pleasant.

I sometimes felt like I was living through a different era of contacts than everyone else. While my friends threw their contacts around, treating them like junk, without consequence, I treated mine like precious heirlooms, only to have my eyes reject their presence again and again. Still, I spent seventeen years trying to make contacts work for me, mostly out of the residual fear that switching to glasses would leave me friendless and alone.

I want to say I've switched to wearing my glasses because I'm no longer concerned about appearing weak. Or because I've entered my thirties and, through this milestone of maturity, I've gotten over worrying about what other people think of me. Or that the very real possibility of living with not just a past symbol of disability, but an actual disability, has finally altered my priorities. But in many ways, the easiest explanation for my change of heart is that the cultural view of them shifted. Glasses may be more fashionable now than at any other moment in their history. Celebrities and models wear them, and sales of frames with nonprescription lenses are at an all-time high. Elementary school kids wear them. Neil Handley, in his observations about the changing social norms of glasses through history, traces the beginning of the relatively recent cultural shift to the popularity of the *Harry Potter* movies. Thanks to that fictional child wizard, there is a new generation of adults who were raised believing that glasses are cool.

Oddly, for most of my life I've thought that other people look better when wearing glasses. Even as I feared the social implications of wearing them, I regularly found myself more attracted to people when they put glasses on. In an unconscious reversal of the movie plot I grew up with, I'm regularly unaware of others' physical beauty until I see them in glasses. And yet, for most of my life, I wasn't able to see myself in the same light. I would put my glasses on and, looking in the mirror, catch sight of the feeble buzzkill I knew I was inside. I saw a guy who didn't want to party as often or as long as everyone else, who liked quiet introspection more than big groups of people, and I deemed these traits unacceptable.

In most areas of my life, I've stopped worrying about strength, weakness, and the related remnants of male socialization that weighed so heavily on me for so long. And I've come to accept, and even like, the bespectacled face that looks back at me in the mirror each day. My glasses have become a part of me. But there are some situations where I still worry about appearing strong. I notice how certain old friends look at me differently now that I wear my glasses every day, how their ideas maybe haven't changed with the culture's, and I wonder why I care. In my head I argue that glasses aren't a weakness: they improve vision and act as a shield for the eyes. I tell myself that it's really the people without glasses—with their unprotected, vulnerable eyes—who are weak.

But even though glasses may be a shield, they're also a mask. A very slight mask, they nonetheless change the shape of the face, disguising the wearer. Even as attitudes around their attractiveness change, statistics demonstrate that people who wear glasses in their online dating profile pictures get passed over more often because, according to sociologist Jess Carbino, glasses obstruct others' ability "to actually look at your face and be able to . . . see your eyes, which are a very strong indicator of trustworthiness." Maybe it's because I'm slow to open up and appreciate the humility of a little hiding, but I relate to David Shields when he writes, "People not wearing glasses sometimes seem preposterously accessible, uncomplicated, unmysterious."

When I reach for my glasses in the morning, I open their arms, bring them to my face, and absorb the weight of their history. I feel the relief they've brought to so many, the stress they've brought to countless others, and centuries of shifting attitudes sit heavy on the back of my earlobes, the bridge of my nose.

[FOUR]

THE IDEA OF DOING NOTHING AT ALL

I IMAGINED A LIFE LIVED EFFORTLESSLY. Not without thought or care, or even work, but a life that didn't look like so many of the lives around me—overextended, drained, trying too hard for too little.

Maybe my fascination with slacking was due in part to the time and place I entered my preteen years: the mid-nineties in rural Washington, less than an hour from Seattle, where a years-in-the-making music scene was reaching the mainstream for the first time. The scene's aesthetic was a rejection of eighties excess, of status symbols and polished surfaces—here was music that was rough around the edges, played by bands dressed in cheap, worn-out clothes. In the years since, it's all been talked to death—the culture's lasting obsession with a guy named Kurt and his little group that has, prophetically, "always been and always will until the end"—but for better or worse, so-called "grunge" was something akin to an unplanned pop-culture revolution, and I was close enough to feel its heat, even if I was too young to be a part of it.

Before this, I didn't think much about my image. Most of my extended family seemed to care little about clothes—choosing comfort and functionality over fashion most of the time—so I'd absorbed that as a value. Even though I drank in absurd quantities of TV, letting every sitcom character and grandiose music-video gesture burn into my retinas, I rarely extended those images to my life or self; the presentations I saw on-screen weren't who I wanted to be, they were just interesting examples of how other people could be.

I started middle school in 1994. I'd turned twelve a few days before classes began, and I was bright-eyed—chubby, redheaded, adorned in a small collection of oversized *Ren & Stimpy* and SuperSonics T-shirts. I loved music, loved everything happening culturally in Seattle, but I still loved sports more. I'd just come out of three years in a low-budget, mixed-grade advanced class that took place in a portable on the playground of our elementary school. The experience had convinced me that I was an overachiever rather than an underachiever. (In retrospect, the class wasn't especially challenging, and had likely been created for oddballs who other teachers thought wouldn't do well, for a wide variety of reasons, in a normal classroom.) Coming out of this small bubble of weirdos I'd lived in for three years, the social dynamics of middle school baffled me, and I quickly retreated back into a shell I'd only recently started coming out of.

And so I listened to music every possible moment, and I watched movies (John Hughes's eighties teen rom-coms, Golden Age screwballs, films of all eras about rebels and outsiders). These movies gave me a taste of the things I longed for as a rural kid with no neighbors who was largely uninterested in rural-kid stuff: the sweet intangibility of cities and suburbs, friends within walking distance, lessons in the fine art of disliking things, and the idea of doing nothing as a way of doing something.

A month into middle school, a movie came out that seemed like it might supply everything I wanted from a movie at the time. Black-and-white, low-budget, following the everyday lives of unmotivated screwups; I still remember Kurt Loder flatly telling me about it on *MTV News*. I couldn't imagine anything I wanted to see more.

Clerks opens with a ringing phone, a dog on a bed, a guy falling out of a closet backwards. He answers the phone, his boss tells him to come into work on his day off, and the movie's series of misadventures begins. Watching it all unfold for the first time, I could feel something shifting inside of me. I remember trying not to blink, afraid I'd miss something—a detail, a bit of wordplay, some clue about life. That the script was largely built on sex jokes didn't matter much to me; what mattered was that the characters talked out their paths and weighed their options, or lack thereof. Though obscured by layers of sarcasm and libido, below the surface I could see they were trying to figure out how best to live life, a question I was just beginning to ask. With repetition, the protagonist's ongoing refrain of "I'm not even supposed to be here today" came to mean something bigger to me, getting right at the heart of the absurdity of our overscheduled, inflexible lives. How could we leave room for being, for enjoying, for becoming, when so much of life was preplanned? The film left me with a pile of questions I happily let rattle around in my head for weeks after. I was hooked.

*

Between 1994 and 1996, there was a particular kind of movie being made that reliably fulfilled all my desires and, because of this, had me under a quiet spell. They were often called slacker movies, and, without much effort, I managed to watch nearly all of them. If I didn't hear about them on MTV or read about them in *Spin*, their boxes called a sweet siren song from the new-release shelves of our small-town video store—boxes featuring disaffected-seeming white boys slouching around with their pampered bedheads and frumpled handsomeness.

These few short years produced full-on star-studded blockbusters depicting underachievers of various shapes and forms, as well as great slacker films that were so well crafted they transcended subgenre (the still-brilliant *Friday* and *Trainspotting*). But the films I was most intrigued by—and the ones that most often received the slacker label—were a dozen movies that played like scene reports, different regional takes on essentially the same thing: unplanned lives, stories told by way of wandering, humor mixing with existential dread. *Clerks*, *Reality Bites*, *Airheads*, *S.F.W.*, *PCU*, *Kicking and Screaming*, *Mallrats*, *Kids*, *Bottle Rocket*, *Empire Records*, *Floundering*, and *SubUrbia.*

These movies didn't have the positivity or charm of *Wayne's World* or *Bill & Ted's Excellent Adventure* from a half decade earlier, or the wit and playfulness of more adult-slacking films—*The Big Lebowski*, *Office Space*, *High Fidelity*—from a half decade later. They were nearly all crass, a bit mean-spirited, the characters self-absorbed and dissatisfied.

I'll admit it now: they don't sound very appealing. And they don't sound like they should have appealed to the person

I was at the time. Though dissatisfied with my rural life and general circumstances, I wasn't mean-spirited or really all that crass. In many of these films, the male roles were nearly interchangeable. Jason Lee in *Mallrats* was Jeremy Piven in *PCU* was Nicky Katt in *SubUrbia*. Stephen Dorff in 1994's *S.F.W.* seemed to be doing a bad impersonation of Ethan Hawke in *Reality Bites*, which had been released seven months earlier. These characters were often depressed, less physically imposing versions of archetypal school bullies—making fun of anyone whose looks or opinions differed from theirs, policing any kind of fun they didn't want to participate in, experts in normalizing casual misogyny and racism—but somehow, the flannels tied around their waists signaled they were different, misunderstood, deep thinkers, secretly sensitive.

For me, this was the first time a media image addressed the suddenly important question of *Who is the person I want to be?* These guys, like my family, seemingly valued clothing for its ability to provide comfort. They reflected a class-based value system I was familiar with, but they also went beyond that, rejecting societal norms surrounding personal aesthetics and work ethics that felt stifling and manufactured. At the time, I believed I was seeing my future self represented on-screen, though on some level I already knew I didn't want to be these guys; they were jerks. Beyond the familiar Pacific Northwest–inspired image, what I saw was really just a piecemeal collection of the kind of traits I wanted to develop in myself: someone who had strong opinions and voiced them confidently, someone who hung out with friends day after day, playing in bands, sitting outside convenience stores, telling stories.

Not long after my first viewing of *Clerks*, everything in my life began to change. I stopped living part-time at my grandparents' house; my single mom got married, got pregnant, and started building a house in front of our trailer. I quit sports—my primary motivator in life up until that point—and started wearing a Sub Pop Records "Loser" shirt to school proudly. By the mid-nineties, the shirt was already a classic, a cliché even, of the Seattle grunge era: big all-caps, white-lettered LOSER on a black shirt. I wore an iron-on patch for the Seattle garage-rock band Gas Huffer centered, without context, on the small pocket of my JanSport backpack, both hoping and dreading that someone might comment on it. I'd excitedly used my lawn-mowing money to buy the T-shirt and patch but felt unsure of my new image once I realized how much attention it drew, and how most of that attention was negative. To others, I wasn't being playfully self-effacing, just confusing.

My favorite song became "Underachievers March and Fight Song," a borderline-novelty song by the band Archers of Loaf, and I sang it under my breath as I took long, aimless walks with my untrained country dog ("Underachievers / Attack at your leisure / Hoist up your guitars / And make them all believers"). I ordered CDs and zines from paper catalogs, recorded songs from the Seattle college station onto cassettes. I tried to imagine the life I would live in the city those songs were broadcast from, forty miles that felt like an entire world away, where the music would soundtrack my days of hanging out without plans, scraping by proudly, living without care.

In retrospect, I can see I was probably struggling with an undiagnosed depression. But at the time, I thought I was just bored. I wasn't exactly upset about all the changes in my life, but I was lost because of them; nothing mattered, but everything mattered too much. I felt that the lack of job opportunities for a thirteen-year-old was infuriating, but work itself was overrated.

My mom had worked two jobs my whole life, and my grandparents had spent their lives in a similarly overworked haze. I saw it in so many of my aunts and uncles and cousins too: this relentless, lower middle-class, pull-up-by-your-bootstraps drive to keep getting by. It's not that I thought my family members were wasting their lives in work, but I knew there had to be something more. I was proud of them, but I could see how much they were sacrificing. On-screen, when families got together, they did fun activities, went on holidays, took ski trips to cabins. When my family got together, we had work parties—clearing brush, spreading gravel, tending the gardens.

I didn't like the idea of giving up life for work, so I appreciated what slacker movies were getting at, in their best moments: interrogating the ideals of the American Dream, examining the shortcomings of defining the self through work, and sowing a general distrust of the typically unquestioned mantra that hard work actually leads to a better life. Though on the weekends I mowed lawns for money and picked up construction and landscaping jobs whenever I could, I imagined this work as a means to an end—a way of one day getting me out of where I was. "Everybody wants to know what's next," Owen Wilson's character says in *Bottle Rocket*, and this notion resonated with me, wrestling as it did with the constant striving to get ahead, being goal-oriented to a fault, always needing the answers. I felt I was different—somehow above the striving. What I really wanted was to just get somewhere I liked and stay there.

*

And yet, within a few years I found I had the same drive as the people who raised me. I picked up more and more under-the-table jobs until I could legally work, then waited tables in a diner throughout high school. At various points in my life, I've treated work as an addiction I had to break, and, in the quarter of a century since my slacker-movie infatuation, I've attempted something close to nothing on a number of occasions. As an adult, I've lived almost exclusively in big group houses, and I've probably spent more time sitting idly on porches than the average employed human.

But I get antsy if my nothing isn't positioned between a lot of something. In general, I've found some kind of middle ground feels best—working hard on labors of love, doing favors for friends, finding ways to work for myself, sidestepping any job that reeks of normality, leaving time to be with the people I care about.

A couple years ago, my various jobs all picked up unexpectedly at the same time. I suddenly felt like my family members from all those decades ago: working multiple jobs, unable to identify where one week ended and the next began. The never-feeling-on-top-of-things state of my life became filled with the same constant, pulsing sense family members had often articulated to me in various ways growing up—that life is work and work never ends until life does. In the face of this realization, I started rewatching slacker movies.

I wanted to remind myself what I'd seen as a preteen and early teen—not just the image, but how I'd imagined my life would be different, how I wouldn't end up in the same spot as the people around me. I knew I probably wouldn't find any grand answers on how to be human in the slacker canon, but I didn't fully anticipate how many cringe-inducing moments I would have to endure. In large part, slacker films haven't aged particularly well. But in each of them I still found something to love, some reason why the film served as a side-door, real-life classroom to me at the time.

It's arguably the genre's namesake, which predated the wave of films that served as the backdrop to my middle-school years, that holds up the best. *Slacker*, Richard Linklater's 1990 film, inspired Kevin Smith to make *Clerks*, and the unexpected success of *Clerks* led to a demand for similar movies, so its predecessor is often viewed as the genre's source material. *Slacker* went to home video in 1992 and, somewhere in my teen-ennui binge, I watched it.

Through the film's baton-pass narrative, the point of view switching from character to character, *Slacker* provides so many different approaches to living one's own life—not exactly outside of society, but not exactly inside of it, either. Musicians, stoners, professors, conspiracy theorists, political activists, amateur filmmakers, and muscle car guys exist alongside people who don't fit into any recognizable category: a television set collector, an elderly man recording questionable philosophical insights into a tape recorder while walking, a gender-ambiguous person peddling Madonna's Pap smear.

"Slackers might look like the left-behinds of society, but they are actually one step ahead, rejecting most of society and the social hierarchy before it rejects them," says Linklater. "The dictionary defines slackers as people who evade duties and responsibilities. A more modern notion would be people who are ultimately being responsible to themselves and not wasting their time in a realm of activity that has nothing to do with who they are or what they might be ultimately striving for."

Though I didn't have the language for it at the time, this is the quality I saw in slacker movies that so appealed to me. While I'm too similar to the people who raised me to be able to relax to the degree slacking requires, I figured out not long after high school that traditional routes don't work for me either. I'm a little stubborn, nothing if not dedicated to my principles, and here I am, decades removed from the me that watched slacker films in a depressed fog, still identifying with the alternate paths these movies explored, even though I no longer believe that doing nothing is particularly cool or admirable. Perhaps *Slacker* works so well for me because it wasn't trying to cash in on a media trend, and the film understood its characters to be working hard, however misguidedly, in their own ways—delving into their passions and preoccupations, absorbed in projects, puzzling out what to make of life on earth, searching for meaning.

Over two decades have passed since I first saw *Clerks*, and my relationship with my own image isn't that different from when I was a preteen: I have a few dozen items of clothing I enjoy, and I rotate through them based on my mood with only the vaguest idea of what any of these simple outfits communicate about me. I generally know if I look sloppy or put together, but I'm largely clueless beyond these broad strokes. I just know it's always important for me to in some way signal that I haven't fully conformed. Even when I dress up for an event, I feel compelled to include one rough-around-the-edges detail—a handkerchief, a notebook in my pocket, sneakers, a weird art shirt under my dress shirt. Something that indicates in the tiniest, most likely imperceptible way that I'm not the professorially preppy grown-up I'm playing the role of, not really.

With all of this on my mind, I go out for a walk. A kid approaches from the other direction—a middle schooler, likely the same age as I was when I first saw *Clerks*—looking like they stepped out of the mid-nineties and into the present moment. They have straight brown hair down to their shoulders, falling in their eyes, an oversized band shirt, and I give them a nod, my curly hair blowing in the wind, my red-and-black flannel open, a band shirt underneath—fully embracing my teenage fashion sense—and I imagine we have a brief connection by way of our shared aesthetic.

I know it's probably not this simple, and that things would have been different if I'd grown up in a different place at a different time, if my family had been white-collar instead of blue-collar, if I'd had different friends, taken a more traditional life path. I can see the mechanisms of image, the reasons this one image seeped into my bones, the reasons I return to it in my thirties, but when I get dressed in the morning, I'm still essentially the kid hunting for slacker movies at the video store: liking what I like because I like it, because it's comfortable, because it's me.

[FIVE]

STARING INTO THE SUN

A BRIEF HISTORY

FOLLOWING A YEARS-LONG BOUT OF AMNESIA at the beginning of the twentieth century—having lived several other lives in several other cities, his wife searching for him in vain until her untimely death—ophthalmologist William Horatio Bates resumed his practice in New York City and began formulating a theory for how the eyes could heal themselves. Bates believed that human eyes, like fish eyes, needed to elongate themselves in order to focus, and he went on to create a series of relaxation techniques that all worked toward the same goal: changing the shape of the eye.

He asked his patients to look at a blank wall without trying to see. To lightly place their palms over their closed lids until they saw perfect blackness. To visualize black letters and black punctuation marks. To stare into the sun. To hold a "burning glass" to enhance the effects of "sunning," or "focusing the sun's rays" upon the eyes. To swing or shift the eyes in precise ways until they achieved "universal swing."

He also encouraged his patients to throw their glasses away. "It is fortunate that many people for whom glasses have been prescribed refuse to wear them, thus escaping not only much discomfort but also much injury to their eyes," he writes, decrying those who "submit to an amount of unnecessary torture which is scarcely conceivable."

Bates was not only opposed to glasses as practical tools, he was disgusted by them. "Some persons have actually come to consider glasses becoming," he laments, before expressing relief that "there are still some unperverted minds to which the wearing of glasses is mental torture and the sight of them upon others far from agreeable. As for putting glasses upon a child, it is enough to make anyone sick at heart."

Bates was a veritable walking proverb:

> "When people are struck down in the street by automobiles or trolley cars, it is often because they are suffering from temporary loss of sight."
>
> "Telling lies is bad for the eyes."
>
> "I have made dogs myopic by inducing them to strain to see a distant object."

He was—brilliantly, beautifully—the quintessential turn-of-the-century quack, throwing known treatments in the trash and forging a new path.

*

If you try to research vision loss in any capacity, you will find William Bates. Sometimes you don't know you're finding him, but he's like Scientology or Ramtha's School of Enlightenment: His basic ideas have quietly embedded themselves into products ready for mass consumption. When I learned about him, I celebrated: a relatively unknown scam artist. *What a find!* I told whoever would listen. *He had people stare into the sun!* I would say, delighted. I spread the gospel of his false gospel. Perhaps my delight was due to the fact that vision loss rarely offers comic relief that isn't mean-spirited. But here it was, in the form of a man, an apparent clown, a joke, or so I thought.

Were he born a century later, Bates's methods would have made him the perfect candidate for the late-night infomercial circuit. I like to imagine it: a room full of people, palms over their eyes, a sonorous voice guiding them toward perfect blackness. Or a line of people, swinging their eyeballs in exact unison, the good doctor cheering them on from the sidelines.

Eventually, I pick up a copy of *The Bates Method for Better Eyesight without Glasses*—the still-in-print posthumous revision of his 1920 book *Perfect Sight without Glasses*—expecting to be delighted all over again by his strange con. And while there are countless absurdities folded into writing, his prose is generally sober and clearheaded. The exclamation points I expected to find littering the pages are nowhere to be found. I'd figured the manipulation would be on the surface, obvious and silly. But if you read him for long enough, it becomes clear: He wasn't a scam artist. He was a believer.

At the core, his methods center around the idea that health issues arise when we don't trust or allow our body to work on its own. In Western culture's emphasis on mind over body we've lost something crucial; now our minds, to our detriment, constantly override our natural functions. To most of his followers it didn't matter if his biological claims were factually accurate or not, because his theories tap into something we all want to believe: that our body knows how to be a body. All his techniques, he argues, "are simply different ways of obtaining relaxation."

Essentially, Bates was selling a bizarre form of meditation—a path to inner peace that begins with the eyes. In his books, he repeatedly reasserts that any sort of effort or strain is the enemy of good vision:

> "Whenever the eye tries to see, it at once ceases to have normal vision."
>
> "[I]n all cases of defective vision a person is unable to see best where he is looking."
>
> "[T]he fact must be stressed that perfect sight can be obtained *only* by relaxation."
>
> "This relaxation cannot, however, be obtained by any sort of *effort*."

Dystopian novelist Aldous Huxley, a follower of the Bates Method, published *The Art of Seeing* in 1942 as a way of getting the Bates Method out of the back of pulp magazines and mail-order catalogs and into the minds of intellectuals. In Huxley's words, "Vision is not won by making any effort to get it: it comes to those who have learned to put their minds and eyes into a state of alert passivity, or dynamic relaxation."

And doesn't that sound nice? Doesn't it seem that—if we could fully, truly, *dynamically* relax—that yes, our vision would be better?

There's no evidence that eye exercises, or any other elements of the Bates Method, work. But Bates was as much a conspiracy theorist as he was a doctor, so a lack of scientific proof to him would have just been viewed as part of a bigger cover-up—one more sign that the powers that be wanted to keep this knowledge from the masses. While his techniques could have gained traction before the early twentieth century, they wouldn't have had much to be opposed to. It was the burgeoning optical industry that infused his exercises with energy. Here was an apparent scam that profited from telling people that their bodies didn't already have the tools they needed. His eye exercises became political statements, tools to work against a corrupt system.

I suspect this is why his ideas have reemerged with such force in recent years. They fit perfectly with the climate of the internet, where science and speculation vie for attention, and often mix so gleefully. If you were to google the phrases "improve vision," "books about corrective lenses," or even, simply, "books about eyesight," most of your results will be descendants of Bates—various people and organizations convinced of the optical industry's shadiness and the hidden potential of the body.

Consider the optometrist appointments, the expensive frames, the piles of boxes filled with disposable contact lenses, how much it all costs. If these books and organizations simply plant the idea in the back of your mind that an entire industry—perhaps even a whole branch of the medical profession—may not need to exist, then their work is not in vain; Bates's ideas spread. And the thing is, after the more absurd parts are stripped away—the morphing shape of the eye, the sun-staring, the burning glass—and some common-sense lifestyle and dietary suggestions are added, it all seems vaguely plausible. I'm not a believer, by any means, but I see why others are. It's all there: a possible conspiracy, a do-it-yourself ethic, a belief in a body that's wise and powerful.

[SIX]

THE BLIND CARTOON

A MAN GOES INTO A GYM, thinking it's a dance school, and waltzes with a punching bag. He enters an airport, thinking it's a movie theater, and ends up on a flight. He stumbles into a military recruitment office, thinking it's a high-end clothing shop, and sets off a grenade. As a kid, I watched *Mr. Magoo* cartoons because they were on, not because I necessarily enjoyed them. In the eighties and nineties, they were a daytime rerun staple on a variety of different cable channels. They filled a void, killing time for both the station and its viewers. Each *Mr. Magoo* cartoon was built on essentially the same gag, played over and over: a low-vision elderly man, too proud to admit the severity of his vision loss, tries to go about normal life unassisted and causes mayhem. Magoo was something distinctly other, a character you never felt sorry for.

*

I've had only one basic recommendation to guide me through my decade of living with recurring retinal hemorrhages: Avoid heavy lifting. It's a general recommendation—there's no weight limit or lift-duration cutoff to follow—which also makes it a vague recommendation. Heavy lifting *could* cause or contribute to a retinal hemorrhage, but there's no proof that it will. It's just a possibility, a guess. But one I'm expected to abide by, just in case.

*

I learned from an early age to establish my worth by how hard I could work. Both my stepdad and my absent biological dad were landscapers. My mom came home from hauling mail and worked outside chopping wood or cutting down brush. I mowed my first lawn for money when I was ten years old; I can't think of a year since when I didn't take on at least one physical labor job for extra cash. I always imagined I would end up being a landscaper, or at least working outside in some capacity. It wasn't what I dreamed of doing, but it seemed inevitable, a destiny I couldn't escape. Like my eye condition, it was something determined at birth and out of my control.

*

I'm ashamed to admit this, but I often feel a bit uncomfortable around people who are blind. Unsure of what to do with my body or voice, I get nervous. This discomfort is somewhat silly because my cousin Joel, who recently passed away, was blind due to diabetes-related complications for over half my life. But even with him—a person I loved dearly and felt at ease talking to—I always had some concerns around the etiquette: Do I announce myself, or does he just know my voice? When I lean in for a hug, do I tell him? When do I describe what he's missing, and when is it insulting to do so? I never asked him these questions because I didn't want to make an issue of his blindness. But now I realize the error in this logic; what could possibly be more caring than asking a person how they would like to be treated? When I interact with blind or low-vision people at events, on the bus, or at the doctor's office, I'm reminded how little I know about their world. I've always been afraid to ask, always avoided real knowledge. Out of this fear, I've allowed representations to fill in the gaps, settling for caricatured notions, cartoon knowledge of human experience.

*

Despite the simplicity of the premise, Mr. Magoo is a surprisingly enduring character. His 1949 debut in *The Ragtime Bear* made him one of the first human cartoon characters—until that point, cartoon characters were almost entirely animals—and the only reason the studio gave the green-light to the project was the presence of a bear. Nevertheless, it turned out that people enjoyed seeing human cartoons, and Magoo quickly became a regular figure in fifties theatrical shorts and the star of one of the first animated television shows in the early sixties (*The Mr. Magoo Show*). The first animated Christmas special came soon after (*Mr. Magoo's Christmas Carol*), followed by another television show in the mid-sixties (*The Famous Adventures of Mr. Magoo*), yet another show in the seventies (*What's New, Mr. Magoo?*), then a live-action feature in the late nineties (*Mr. Magoo*), and a long stint as an animated spokesman for an optical company in the mid-aughts. And yet, his endurance has always baffled me, since I've never met anyone who claimed to be a fan of the cartoon. Even his creators, aware of the gag's limitations, wanted to retire the character after his first appearance.

*

My current eye doctor doesn't talk about the future. When I try to bring it up, he pulls back. The treatment is working now, why would I want to worry about it not working? My old eye doctor considered everything an unknown, the treatment a bandage. He was sure that one day I'd go blind, that all we could do was hold it at bay. This was in the treatment's early years, so perhaps he feels differently now that it has a more proven track record, but I still shoulder his dread. Sometimes I wonder if I'm being extreme, worrying before I need to. But then my retina will hemorrhage, and I'll wonder if I'm not worrying enough.

*

A couple years ago, an acquaintance hired me to help him with a moving job. In addition to working for a moving company in my early twenties, I'd helped dozens of friends move over the years, so I felt confident taking the job. Though I knew it was hypothetically risky given my eye condition, I needed the money.

In large part, the job felt great. But it was more work than my acquaintance had anticipated, and we found ourselves under a time crunch. I'd warned him beforehand that I couldn't lift anything too heavy, but in our rush this became impossible to hold to, and I carried things that I knew were probably risky—large potted trees, glass tables, metal lawn sculptures—feats my doctor would have certainly described as "heavy lifting." I felt, with each item, the slight pressure behind the eyes—a pressure I never used to notice—that occurs when the body tenses to withstand a weight.

Within a week I began to sense a familiar fuzzy spot in my central field of vision. For days I cleaned my glasses, testing myself by reading business signs or studying the small creases on a person's face. But then the fuzzy spot grew, shapes began taking on dramatic angles, and my internal organs turned, knowing I had worked against my body.

I probably would have written off the whole episode as a coincidence if the same thing hadn't happened the previous year when I'd moved my own belongings. In a hurry and not wanting to inconvenience anyone, I loaded up the moving truck by myself. Within a couple weeks, my world began to blur and take on a kaleidoscopic quality—a fun house–mirror effect that I've come to recognize as the beginning of my for-now-treatable vision loss.

*

Originally, Mr. Magoo's vision was metaphorical. Conceived by Communist Party–affiliated animators, they created Magoo to represent the McCarthyist type of man who was blind to his prejudices, shortsighted in his goals, lacking vision. Blindness and vision-related metaphors like these are embedded so deeply in the English language that we don't notice most of them. We have blind spots, wear blinders, and the blind lead the blind as we turn a blind eye. Few of these embedded metaphors are positive—"blind luck" is about as good as it gets, and even that has an implied dopiness. Meanwhile, we applaud those who are insightful, farsighted visionaries who have an eye for eye-opening opportunities. This sort of language is so pervasive that, regardless of the intent behind it, the conclusions are undeniable: In our society, sight is celebrated while blindness is feared.

*

Though I like being helpful, I often don't feel comfortable being helped. Part of this discomfort developed out of the gender expectations I grew up with in rural America. I may have learned to do jobs that required physical labor, but I've never been particularly inclined toward fixing or building things. I've worked on construction crews, cutting hundreds, even thousands of boards, but I wouldn't feel the least bit confident building anything out of wood. Nor out of any material, really. Being a not-so-handy man growing up in a place where men were expected to be adept at fixing things and to have an understanding about the inner workings of machines, I learned early on that if you don't ask for help, few people will notice your ineptitude. As much as I've tried to evolve past it, I still feel uneasy about asking for help, ashamed to admit that I can't do something on my own.

*

After the moving job, I finally acknowledged that I was contributing to my vision loss by being careless. So I vowed to stop taking physical labor jobs, even though it felt like I was giving up something essential to my being—the death of a way of life. But even now, I still catch myself wondering about my value if I can't chip in when needed. Who am I if I can't physically help a friend in need or contribute to a job that needs to get done? I'm sure by most people's standards it sounds like a silly loss—who wouldn't want an excuse to get out of backbreaking work?—but lifting heavy things is, almost as much as having sight, a part of my identity.

*

A few years ago, my cousin Joel and I realized that we'd received the same then-experimental treatment. I was stunned to learn that someone I knew and loved could relate to what I'd been going through, and we talked excitedly, comparing experiences and laughing about the horror-movie awfulness of watching a needle getting stuck into your own eye. Here was the perfect opportunity to ask the bigger questions I'd always wanted to ask, the ones that might someday be important for me to know. How did he experience the world? What were the unexpected challenges, the unknown blessings? How did he transition from being an independent adult to being the youngest person in a nursing home? And how, exactly, did he become so okay with being helped? But it was a holiday, we were surrounded by family who were curious about our sudden excitement, and I felt embarrassed. I don't like having the spotlight on me in casual situations, especially when I'm asking another person to be vulnerable with me. So, as soon as the marvel of the coincidence wore down, I changed the subject.

*

Throughout my life I've repeatedly made myself uncomfortable to avoid asking for help. On car trips as a kid, I would hold my pee in for hours, hoping someone else would eventually need to go to the bathroom. I still find myself doing this as an adult. Rather than delay whoever I'm with, I've skipped meals, skipped coffee, skipped changing my clothes, skipped showers, and skipped sleep. I'm trying to change this inclination to please, but the possibility that one day I'll need constant assistance is still one of my biggest fears. An even bigger fear is that I just won't ask for it.

I don't have a significant other or children, and all my closest friends and family members live in other cities. No one would be required to take care of me and, given my condition, it would likely be a slow fade—a gradual decrease in one eye and then the other—rather than a sudden emergency. I imagine myself becoming Magoo, stumbling into situations, pretending everything's fine. A clumsy joke, alone.

It's natural to assume that if I lose a significant amount of my vision, I'll reach out for help. I'll turn to friends, I'll take a white cane training program, I'll get instructed in various assistive technologies. And I hope that's what happens. But I know my tendencies. Over a year ago I injured my wrist; several months later I injured my back. Since then, I've asked for help once or twice and told friends I couldn't help them two or three times. Both of these injuries have limited my abilities, and neither has healed because I keep doing everything myself, not even mentioning to others that these issues exist.

*

It's perhaps telling that the 1997 live-action feature starring Leslie Nielsen as Magoo was boycotted widely by disability-rights organizations; the main gag became too obviously insensitive when taken out of the animated realm. Thanks to this boycott, it became increasingly apparent that Magoo had always been offensive. "The misunderstandings of blindness caused by the Magoo character have bedeviled the lives of thousands of blind people," the president of the National Federation of the Blind said at the time. "Magoo" was once a common insult lobbed at blind and nearsighted people, often extending to the spacey, clumsy, and accident-prone. Kids who grew up blind during the height of Magoo's popularity often speak about the damage the character did to their self-esteem. The issues they ran into and accidents they had didn't inspire sympathy but instead were viewed as comedy, their problems something to laugh at. Even today, most people consider Mr. Magoo innocuous, and I wonder why gags about people who are blind are still so acceptable. Is it because the sighted consider the world of the blind—a realm without our most relied-upon sense—a distinctly separate universe?

*

There are days when I walk around thinking about what I might miss most. Sometimes it seems likely that it'll be the practical benefits of sight, such as the ability to pick up on facial cues. Other times I'm convinced that it will be the moments of natural beauty, like when sunlight lands on top of a body of water in a previously unknown-to-me way. I think about how losing my sight could change my life as a writer. How it might change the way I experience sexual attraction, and the way I relate to a world that's increasingly image driven. Some of my discomfort around people who are blind comes from being confronted with an image of my future self. *Someday this will be you*, I think, as I speak too loudly, make pointless gestures with my hands—simultaneously fearing the image and trying to figure out how I might embrace it.

[SEVEN]

ONE OF THE STYLES OF LIVING

A CONVERSATION SERIES

This series uses only the words of the interview subjects, edited down from our longer recorded conversations.

M. LEONA GODIN: writer, performer, educator, author of *There Plant Eyes: A Personal and Cultural History of Blindness*

"There's always been blind writers; I feel what there hasn't been is a blind-writer community. And I feel like it's so important—it's the next step, right? I think if we just have a singular blind voice every few years that it kind of ends up bludgeoning everybody else. There's something about community that makes it possible to unravel that inspirational narrative, that overcoming narrative.

"Sometimes it happens that a singular blind voice rises, and there's this implicit understanding that they have overcome blindness in order to become a writer, and they've done something that is quite extraordinary as a blind person. And that becomes the overarching narrative.

"So instead of realizing that blindness is part of who we are—so there are many many many blind narratives—the tendency of mainstream culture is to want to celebrate a singular one, then be like, 'okay, bye bye,' and to not actually have the mainstream move in the direction of blindness. It's like, 'Oh, that's a nice story; now we don't need to think about a blind person for a little while.'

"It's been really important for me to recognize how having a career as a blind writer basically necessitates me helping and connecting with other blind writers. As opposed to being like, 'Look at me! Look at how I've overcome this thing you all despise.' There's something fundamentally ableist, yes, but kind of self-hating in that story. Finding blind community in the writer world—and in the artistic world more generally—is vital for us to get to the next phase of actually having careers as writers.

"Even someone like James Joyce—he's basically never taught from the perspective of blindness. This is something I'm thinking a lot about as a teacher. I don't know how many classes I've taken about John Milton—it wasn't until I was doing a little extra reading for the *Paradise Lost* chapter of my book that I finally came across the word 'disability.' People have this idea that when we teach Joyce, when we teach Milton, we think of them as so singular that it doesn't affect the blind community. The scholars that are teaching Joyce and Milton are not thinking about them in terms of community, they're thinking about them in terms of the genius who happens to have been struck blind.

"From the beginning, I knew I did not want to write a

memoir. And it wasn't because I don't adore memoirs. Because I do. It's just that that's what everyone wants from the blind writer, or blind figures of any kind. And I think this goes for disability more generally: People want that personal narrative. But that's only one aspect of it, because they only want the memoir. And that's where things get very dangerous. If we're always pushed to write memoirs and we're not allowed to write anything else, then nothing changes. The implicit suggestion is: That's all we can write about. That's the danger. Again, obviously I love memoirs and I love all the blind memoirs I mention in my book, but I worry that it lets mainstream culture off the hook too easily."

"I like to put words on the page fast and then it's all about the edit. I'm no different than a lot of writers in that way. I know there are writers who do the opposite and labor over every sentence, but I'm not that kind of writer. I'm definitely a 'get me out of the blank page as quickly as possible' kind of writer. Even if I know that 80 percent, or even more, is going to be totally cut or rearranged, it always gives me a huge relief to know I've gotten the words on the page.

"I do the bulk of my writing or typing into a regular laptop, and then I have text-to-speech software reading stuff back to me—either slowly or quickly or by the sentence or by the line or the paragraph. So the sound of my sentences has become very important to me. But in recent years, as I've been trying to do more with braille, that's changed a little bit for me. One funny thing that happened in the reading of the audiobook for *There Plant Eyes* is that I was like, 'Man, I write some long sentences!' That's one of those things where—because I'm not considering the eye, the need for that rest for the eyeball, the period—I think I've not been super kind to my readers. It probably didn't help that I came out of an academic writing career either. So I think that'll change the more I read braille because I feel like I'm aware of different things.

"For readings, I use what I've dubbed 'the Cyrano method,' where a little earbud is in my ear and I basically repeat what Cyrano the electronic voice says. I cut my lines very short, so I can have a lot of control over the speed and how I read it. But I did my audiobook with an earbud in, and it was rough. The director and I had some issues in the middle of it where we were like, 'Oh my god, we're not going to be able to finish this,' but by the end I was apparently reading at a professional speed—which is about seventeen pages an hour. But it was quite an experience.

"There's something about disability—because of its very potential to touch everybody's lives—that makes it so people are resistant to the idea of disability pride in a way that they're not for other pride movements. It's one of these great ironies—that you could become a part of this identity, or a part of this group of people, at any moment—that this should be one that people feel so resistant towards. It's deep-seated; I don't know how to explain it. And how do we get around it? This is a baseline, visceral fear people have about disability—and about blindness in particular."

[EIGHT]

CAPTURED

BY THE TIME I REACHED HIGH SCHOOL, despite having dedicated most of my preteen and early teen years to sports, I still—at least internally—held on to the identity I had established as a preschooler, when I'd decided I was an artist. I still remembered the self that woke up every morning, climbed on the stool at the kitchen counter, and went to work with my watercolors and crayons like it was a job. That kid with an obsessive drive and artistic vision was still me. It didn't matter that my abilities were stuck at the level of a child, the sense of myself as an artist held strong.

It's difficult to be an artist when you have no skills in any artistic discipline. But I kept trying things out, hoping something would stick. When a darkroom photography class was offered my junior year, I signed up. Like writing, photography was a thing most people were able to do that could also become an art. That possibility—the ordinary transforming into the extraordinary—attracted me. I didn't exactly understand how that transformation happened, but I wanted to find out.

Like so many young, aspiring photographers, I fell in love with Robert Frank's 1958 book *The Americans*. Backed by a Guggenheim Fellowship, the Swiss-born Frank drove across the United States in the mid-fifties and, over the course of nine months, traveled ten thousand miles through thirty states, going through 767 rolls of film and taking twenty-seven thousand photos. Those twenty-seven thousand got whittled down to the eighty-three that became the book's raw and perfectly baffling assortment of images.

I loved how Frank took the cultural cues of Americana and turned them questionable and strange. A cowboy lighting a cigarette against a garbage can on a dirty city street. A grumpy diner waitress standing below a horrific image of Santa Claus and a sign for jumbo-size hot dogs. A woman in a window, her face obscured by an American flag. A vacant gas station in the desert with a large sign that just says SAVE.

I loved how the photos in *The Americans* caught people with their masks off. The images were so unlike most of the photos of people I'd seen before then, with all their forced smiles and awkward attempts at hiding awkwardness. Frank's photos, I felt, were real. They revealed something hidden—in both the people and the country.

When I learned *The Americans* was part of a movement or style called street photography, I began making my way through the library's photography section, trying to find more of it. Frank's melancholic American road-trip photos led me to Walker Evans's claustrophobic New York City subway photos, which led me to Garry Winogrand's aggressive shots of New York City streets, which led me to André Kertész's geometric studies of silhouetted figures on Parisian streets, which led me to Henri Cartier-Bresson's streets the world over. I loved it all. This, I decided, was what I would one day do.

Unfortunately, my least favorite English teacher doubled as the photography teacher. He liked talking about how, if we practiced hard enough, we could one day work at the portrait studio in the mall. Even if I'd had a different teacher, there would have remained so many things about the class I didn't like—the way we crowded into the darkroom together, everyone watching over your shoulder, the fact that we had to stay after school to get anything significant done.

But my biggest issues with photography occurred outside the classroom and the darkroom. As a shy, overly polite teen, it was difficult for me to point a camera at someone's face, even when my subject was aware of what I was doing and willing to participate. I'd imagined photography would be a way for me to reveal my view of the world to the world, but I hadn't thought about what that revelation entailed. It wasn't as simple as it looked in Frank's photos—the casualness and apparent ease turned out to be an illusion.

So I opted to take pictures of coffee-mug handles and train rails, stacks of bricks and chair shadows. Even then, I had to deal with other people. Each time I took a picture in public, there was someone asking what I was doing while I was doing it. I told myself that these people just couldn't imagine the ordinary transformed. The truth was that I didn't want to admit the obvious: Taking a picture of a cup will make anyone look like a fool, regardless of their inner vision. These days, watching others hovering their phones over their brunch plates, I can't help but look down on them. *How can you judge?* I ask myself. *This was once you, in a way.* I try to convince myself it's somehow different—I was after art while they're after likes—but that's maybe just another story I tell myself.

Filmmaker Wim Wenders says that he's "in search of a new word for this new activity that looks so much like photography, but isn't photography anymore." In the age of latté roses, mirror selfies, and screenshots, I understand Wenders's argument: There is something different, something other about the current manner in which people visually document the world. It borrows aspects from art photography, advertising photography, photojournalism, and point-and-shoot casualness, while not quite being any of those things. But photography has always encompassed so many styles that Wenders's statement also seems silly, snobbish. Photography has always resisted being any one thing, resisted being an art, resisted being something that can be universally held in high regard. Making any broad statement about photography is bound to come up short, because photography is so much.

Photography is Sears portraits, gallery art, journalism, and porn. It's a mountain range at sunrise, an abstract pattern on the surface of a body of water, a small rodent approaching extinction, a wool sweater on a handsome model.

It's bacteria on a petri dish, bodies at a crime scene, stars forming in the Eagle Nebula. It's framed portraits on the mantle, old *Life* magazine special issues at the thrift store, dusty albums on the bookshelf, the headshots of aspiring actors, Instagram feeds, Facebook profiles, press photos. It's weddings, graduations, and the first day of school. It's disposable cameras, point-and-shoots, XLRs, Polaroids, medium and large formats, but now mostly phones. It honors, it exploits, it educates, it turns us on and turns us off. "Photography evades us," Roland Barthes writes. "We might say that photography is unclassifiable."

In community college, I did a photo series in twenty-four-hour grocery stores late at night, photographing my stoned friends examining fruit. I shot from the hip at checkout lines, parked myself at the automatic doors, and tried to embrace the endless rows of overbearing fluorescents. As if doing a project in the least ideal lighting conditions wasn't already challenging enough, I decided to expose the images with transparency overlays where, in my childish scrawl, I scratched in lines of poetry I'd written. The result looked like an accident: barely legible words, existing without explanation at the bottom of each print. I liked it, put a lot of thought and time into it, but to most people it was more or less unintelligible. I should have started with something simpler, something straightforward, but I couldn't allow myself to be a beginner. I had too many ideas for that.

I did a photo series of my friend in his garage, hood up on his car, shop-light playing off the metal, contrasted against the surrounding darkness. I spent the entire session underneath, hidden, shooting up through the gaps between the block and the hoses. This is where I was most comfortable—with one other person, in a private location, the subject at ease, doing something they loved. During these years, Walker Evans's words were a mantra I prominently displayed in my journal: "Stare, pry, listen, eavesdrop. Die knowing something. You are not here long." His encouragement inspired me to be brave, to put myself out there without worrying how others responded. Deep down, though, I didn't want to pry or stare, didn't want to make people uncomfortable. I wanted to soothe, to calm, to assist in helping another person lower their guard. But here was the problem: As far as I was concerned, artists didn't work like this. This was the terrain of yearbook and wedding photographers—necessary roles, sure, but never imbued with the importance and romance of art. I tried to ignore the fact that my skills were likely more suited to the mall portrait studio than the art world. I tried to push myself out of my comfort zone, but every time I picked up a camera I questioned who I was.

It's hard for me to read Evans's words now without stumbling over the selfishness of his approach, the inherent privilege embedded within. Having read interviews with him, I've come to recognize that he was a playful person, good at saying things for effect, and to take him too literally is to miss the subtle smirk underneath this advice. But it's hard to completely shrug off what he's suggesting: knowing you can stare and get away with it, that you can pry without worrying—without having to worry—how it will make others feel.

“There is an aggression implicit in every use of a camera,” Susan Sontag writes. It was this aggression that made me question myself each time I put the viewfinder to my eye, attempting to capture an image. I was not only *taking* a photo, I was *shooting* someone.

Among my friends, Hannah was the best photographer. She was forceful, brazen, confident—everything I wished I was. She didn’t worry about the silly concerns I obsessed over, didn’t overanalyze the verbs we use for photographing the world. She just put herself and her camera out there. She brought it to every event and didn’t mind that it changed the air in the room, that it made people squirm. She was able to make art out of otherwise uneventful parties, knowing that everyone would be happy later, when the pictures were developed and the moment was in the past. She was sure that everyone would forget how their bodies tensed up, how the camera made conversation difficult—that we would simply remember the idealized moment within the photograph. Which is exactly what happened. Her photos gave us an instant nostalgia for events that often hadn’t even been that great. But through her eyes, we wanted to live them again.

I wished I could acknowledge the trade that Hannah made so easily: the moment for the artifact, the life lived for the art. But I was too aware of how the presence of a camera changed a room—how the camera in my hands kept me from fully participating in life, that to put a camera to your eye is to observe rather than to join.

I did a photo series in an abandoned garden center that sat on a semirural stretch of road with nothing nearby. My friends and I liked to sneak in. We always went late at night, beers in our backpacks, already tipsy, and climbed on the mountains of trash, avoiding broken glass and breaking more in the process. During these trips I became fascinated with the accumulation, the mass of stuff. Nothing had been packed and hauled off when the garden center closed years earlier, it was all just fenced in and left for the weeds to cover, left for the punk kids to break down the remaining pieces of its existence.

Going during the day was a different experience. Not as charged with mystery—just a lonely place filled with a dream that didn't work out. The sheer amount of stuff was perfect for late-night exploring, but, when peering through the camera's tiny frame in the late afternoon, I found it to be overwhelming. I didn't know how to capture it all. I brought friends with me and had them wander around to give some humanity to all the objects. Still, I didn't know what to focus on. There was just so much.

Though I tried to pretend my various photo series were documenting real events and places—the world of grocery stores in the middle of the night, a friend at work in his garage, an abandoned garden center—my main subjects for these projects were essentially models. They were manufactured, inorganic, placed. They wouldn't have been there without me asking them to be there, and it showed.

Pretend like you're not in front of a camera, went the advice, but this tainted so many otherwise wonderful photographs: the act. The only way around it, I felt, was to sneak shots, to not let your subject know they were a subject. *Be like the street photographers*, I told myself. *Be daring and clever, stop caring*. But I couldn't.

*

Google "street photographers" and you'll notice a common thread: Regardless of which segments of the population they're known for photographing, the photographers themselves are almost uniformly white, and predominantly men. In the top ten search results, there are only three women, and one of them, Vivian Maier, has only become known in the past decade, years after her death. In the top forty results, there are only three people of color.

There's an undeniable privilege in being able to look. And even though I couldn't articulate it at the time, this was part of my discomfort during my attempts to be a photographer. In those efforts, I was asserting my privilege in a way that was loud and undeniable, decidedly different from how I typically moved through the world, and I didn't like how it felt.

Having read biographies and watched documentaries about my favorite street photographers, I'm aware that the majority, while considering themselves artists first and foremost, also saw their work as a way to spread empathy—to ask viewers to consider the humanity of people very different from themselves. Most seem to have been in part guided by Lewis Hine's turn-of-the-century notion of "social photography," an attitude perhaps best summarized by historian Alan Trachtenberg: "A picture was a piece of evidence, a record of social injustice, but also of individual human beings surviving with dignity in intolerable conditions." From the perspective of these street photographers, they were using their privilege for good.

But they were also well aware of the discomfort they caused, their own forcefulness. Frank puts it most succinctly when he says that, as a street photographer, "you intrude." Cartier-Bresson, a self-proclaimed humanist, describes his technique as a street photographer using the words "prowl," "pounce," "trap," and "seize." These words, while not terribly offensive, still emphasize the inherent moral ambiguity in taking photos of strangers. While their pictures remain more surprising, more emotionally open than almost any other photographs I know of, I wonder: What about the people in the photographs? Was it an honor for them to be represented in this way? Or a burden?

Having photographed a lot of people, I know that the subject mostly focuses on their own image in the end product. And, of course, it's difficult to look objectively at a photo of yourself. You look past the frame, the lighting—really, the composition as a whole—and go straight to your face. You focus on your open pores, your mussed hair, the lines around your mouth. It's not art, it's you.

After I set my camera down, I remembered how to be present in the moment. I stopped feeling guilt for taking a photo, guilt for not taking a photo. I stopped thinking about what life would look like later, when it was printed out and hung on a wall. I stopped worrying about what I wasn't capturing on film and remembered what it was like to just have an experience. I was twenty-two years old and very concerned about having experiences. I didn't want to miss anything. Capturing one moment, I realized, meant missing so many others.

One day, not long after I decided to stop trying to be a photographer, I took a walk in the woods with a friend. Instead of mentally framing a shot that he was in, I saw him. I noticed his shy eyes, his mind searching for something bigger he didn't yet have words for, the depth of his intelligence—aspects of him I had previously missed. If anything, I learned more from quitting photography than from practicing it.

The well-known street photographers of today tend to be more respectful. They're in large part fashion photographers, or casual sociologists, and we typically know them by their photo blog or Instagram project rather than their name—*Humans of New York*, *Tune*, *The Sartorialist*. And while I appreciate this work, it seems to me that these photographers are sharing concepts more than particular artistic visions. Their photos lack what initially attracted me to Frank or Evans—or what I love about Maier, with her secretive box camera, held at the stomach instead of to the eye—these contemporary street photographers don't capture people with their guards down.

In the majority of today's popular street photography, people pose. And there's power in the well-posed photo. I love when I can see that brief relationship between the subject and the photographer, or simply the relationship between the subject and the camera's lens. Posed photos carry both the idea of self that the subject wants to project and the self the subject can't hide. But they don't move me like candid photos do—photos where the subject is open, messy, full of life. "Once somebody's aware of the camera, it becomes a different picture," observes Frank. "People change."

And I can see how something is lost when they're treated with this particular kind of respect. When I look at popular street photography today, I see people with their masks on.

In this era, where so much is being documented and everyone's a street photographer with their own gallery wall and audience, I often wonder about the lines between privacy and documentation, respect and art. I still want to see people photographed with their guards down, their masks off, showing me a vulnerability I believe we all share and carry within us, but one that most of us look past when we walk the streets. My well of empathy is deeper because of *The Americans*, because of Cartier-Bresson and Evans and Maier. But I don't know if I believe the world is up for grabs, that people in public are available subjects simply because they're in public. I don't know if I ever did.

[NINE]

CONTACT

A CATALOG

LOOKING ANOTHER PERSON IN THE EYES. Why isn't it easier, given that many of us have countless chances each day to practice? Maybe it's the sheer amount we encounter, the deluge of eyes, that makes it so challenging; perhaps the overload is what makes us each so sure one moment and so unsure the next.

* *
* *

Over the past decade, as I've received regular treatments to limit vision loss, I've begun paying closer attention to how we use our eyes, what we take for granted, what's easy and what's difficult. I keep coming back to eye contact. How people struggle with it in such a wide variety of ways, often without realizing they're struggling. Meeting some eyes, ignoring others. All the things eye contact can mean or say: emotional vulnerability, kindness, stability, cruelty, whether we're telling truths or telling lies.

* *
* *

Those of us who live in cities see strangers in greater numbers than people we know. Walking down the street, how do we choose who to make eye contact with and who to look past? When to keep our eyes forward—staring into the future, focused on our own path and no one else's—and when to acknowledge our crossing paths?

* *
* *

Eye contact is the most basic way we acknowledge and connect with one another. But it's also a tool for intimidation, manipulation, and control. I often wonder about the lines between these extremes. Is there a universally respectful gaze? One that no person would interpret as even slightly manipulative or spiteful? Each instance of eye contact is differentiated by slight facial gestures, the momentary and shifting arrangement of tiny muscles around the eyeball, the interpretation of which will vary depending on the culture and the person.

* *
* *

Sociologist Erving Goffman terms brief eye contact, nods between strangers, and similar actions of semi-engagement as "civil inattention." We demonstrate our civility not just by looking at one another, but also by looking away—since the latter lets the other person know we aren't going to violate their personal space or break any social norms. The term itself sounds negative, and given that it's describing spaces—buses, waiting rooms, elevators—where we act as if we're "alone together," it suggests a social ill, a place where we have failed at basic humanity. But ultimately, isn't that what most of us typically want—to be left alone but, somehow, not be lonely?

* *
* *

In her book *Don't Let Me Be Lonely*, poet Claudia Rankine writes:

> In my dream I apologize to everyone I meet. Instead of introducing myself, I apologize for not knowing why I am alive. I am sorry. I am sorry. I apologize. In real life, oddly enough, when I am fully awake and out and about, if I catch someone's eye, I quickly look away. Perhaps this too is a form of apology. Perhaps this is the form apologies take in real life.

* *
* *

It seems wrong to not acknowledge the many people I pass by each day. So, in many cases, I look at them briefly, then look to the ground. In my mind, it's a gesture of respect—a form of bowing, perhaps. A combination of a greeting and a sign of deference. On the other hand, considering the range of possible meanings, what does the other person see? I always hope they see the respect I intend, but I suspect that, more often than not, people see a lack of confidence or an apparent disinterest. Maybe even a refusal to acknowledge them, a sign of disrespect. Given the room for interpretation, I sometimes wonder if it's worth looking at others at all.

* *
* *

It's difficult to figure out how long to hold a polite gaze, a moment of acknowledgment. A study at University College London found that people are generally comfortable with 3.2 seconds of eye contact from a stranger—advice that seems impossible to employ—but are comfortable with longer intervals when they think the person (somehow) looks "trustworthy."

* *
* *

The Everything Body Language Book says that "normal" eye contact is to "hold the gaze for a few seconds, look away, repeat." *The Power of Eye Contact* recommends, depending on the situation—whether a date, business meeting, or customer service interaction—a series of slightly differently timed intervals between holding and looking away. Reading eye-contact advice, it's difficult to ignore how these unnatural, timed actions are supposed to fool others into believing we're acting naturally.

* *
* *

Some pieces of eye-contact advice are overly detailed, even confusing. Consider this suggestion from *A Novice's Guide to Speaking in Public*: "Dividing the room into sections A, B, and C gives the speaker a plan for moving his eyes in a pattern rather than randomly scanning or moving indiscriminately around the room. The speaker makes eye contact with section A of the room and depending on the speaker's skill and poise she may pick out one or two audience members who have reciprocal smiles or otherwise seem to connect with the speaker. Then the speaker can choose to move to section B, and then C."

* *
* *

Other pieces of eye-contact advice seem too vague to be useful. In response to the question, "What is the proper eye contact for a salesperson?" professional sales trainer Tony Alessandra answers, "Intermittent. You definitely want to have solid eye contact. But you should be wary of overdoing it, just as you should be wary of underdoing it."

* *
* *

When I talk to friends about eye contact, I hear repeatedly that figuring out which eye to look at is a constant struggle—something I'd never consciously thought about, and therefore hadn't, until now, struggled with. Since focusing on two separate points simultaneously is not actually possible, we typically find ourselves looking into only one eye, or darting between the two. Most books recommend spending ten seconds at a time on each eye. Some guides suggest widening your gaze, taking in the person's whole face, and just letting their eyes rest in your central field of vision. Others suggest focusing on the bridge of a person's nose, or an eyebrow, to create the illusion of eye contact.

* *
* *

In my nine years of working as a used-book buyer at an independent bookstore, I saw a wide range of fetish-book buys—all types of specialized erotica fiction, photography books, fantasy art, and countless rounds of John Norman's women-as-space-captives sci-fi mass-markets. Awkward interactions following these buys were common, and nearly all these customers avoided looking at me when I explained which ones I bought and which I passed on. I knew something personal about their lives, and they didn't want to see this knowledge in my eyes.

* *
* *

An enduring trope in pop music is to look into the eyes of a lover or love interest and receive a message, clear as day. "Just one look," Doris Troy sings, distilling the essence of all eye-related communication in song, "and I fell so hard." Diana Ross, telling the story of a lover who refuses to speak with her, sings, "But when the love-light starts shining through his eyes / Made me realize how he felt inside." Other singers claim to see forever, to catch glimpses of heaven, paradise, the doorway to a thousand churches. Maybe I should accept these assertions just like I joyously accept so many other hyperbolic statements in song. But while I used to buy into the romance of this sort of thing when I was younger, now I think, *Isn't that just bad communication? Lack of proper consent?*

* *
* *

Due to Mandy Len Catron's viral-to-the-point-of-absurdity *Modern Love* essay, "To Fall in Love with Anyone, Do This," many people now believe four minutes of silent eye contact is essential for falling in love. On Catron's first date with her then future husband, the two tried out aspects of psychologist Arthur Aron's interpersonal closeness studies: thirty-six questions that build in emotional intensity, followed by a period of silent eye contact. In the studies, the eye contact was given less importance and ranged from two to four minutes, but Catron popularized it as "exactly four minutes." When asked about this, she explained, "Two minutes is just enough to be terrified. Four really goes somewhere."

* *
* *

In the mid-2000s, eye-gazing parties had a brief moment of popularity. Like speed dating without talking, participants silently gazed into a stranger's eyes for three minutes before moving on to another stranger, and another, and another. Reporting on an early eye-gazing party for *Slate*, Jennifer DeMeritt observed that the parties "didn't reveal compatibility so much as extroversion."

* *
* *

Many psychologists consider eye contact a quick test to tell if someone is an extrovert or introvert. "Extroverts usually make really good eye contact with you while they're talking, and tend to look around more when they're listening," writes author Mike Bechtle. "Introverts tend to break eye contact when they're the ones talking, but give solid eye contact when they're listening." So perhaps my interest in eye contact—or even the fact that I notice it at all—is simply because I'm an introvert. All my life I've watched extroverted eyes wander when I talk. When this happens, I can't help but wonder if I'm a boring person or if my companions are just easily distracted. If I have to think about what I'm saying—remember details, form an opinion, find the right words to express a thought—I almost always look away. I stare into the distance, slightly to the side of my listener's face, wondering why I can find the words there but not in my listener's eyes.

* *
* *

At the bookstore, I saw all manner of books about eye contact, and I eventually came to the conclusion that most of them are, in some way, creepy. Books that focus on eye contact are typically written for those who don't just want to make eye contact, but who want to use eye contact to get what they want. I would wager that most sincere, down-to-earth people don't typically study eye contact. Yet, to better understand it, I felt I had to. While reading these books on the bus, I hid the covers. At home, I read them cooped up in my room, away from my roommates. I feared that if they saw me reading these books, our interactions might change; they might reappraise my way of looking at them as being insincere, perhaps even a way for me to assert dominance. I was on guard each time I brought these books into public, avoiding contact while reading about how to make it.

* *
* *

Some recently published eye-contact books:

The Ultimate Eye Contact Mastery: Practical Guide to Glow in Confidence, Attract People and Excel in Work and Life with Your Powerful Eyes

The Alpha Male's Guide to Mastering the Art of Eye Contact

Eye Contact Training: How to Attract and Seduce a Woman, Increase Your Confidence and Become a Leader

* *
* *

For most of my life, my closest friends have been women. When I'm walking with them, I observe the near-constant aggressive attempts at eye contact they receive, and they often tell me stories about the small, everyday ways men are inappropriate with them. Because of this, when walking on my own, I often look away from women, simply because I don't want to come off as a creep. I don't want to contribute to this, don't want a nod intended to be polite to be misconstrued. Sometimes I feel guilty for being attracted to a person, and I look away to apologize. *Sorry for my eyes*, I'd like the gesture to say.

* *
* *

At one point in *The Power of Eye Contact*, after trying to woo an uninterested woman for ten years, author Michael Ellsberg tries once again after studying the intricacies of eye contact. He writes, "This time I had a new weapon in my arsenal . . . *eye gazing*," capturing precisely the kind of predatory attitude I associate with studying eye contact.

* *
* *

Early on in life, I learned that I could largely steer clear of bullies and kids looking for a fight by avoiding making eye contact with them. Kids who wanted to fight often used eye contact as an invitation, an excuse to prey on those unsuspecting enough to meet their gaze. But I learned to prepare for it, to be an expert in avoiding contact.

* *
* *

In her article on "visual violence," psychologist Shelagh Robinson writes, "Hate eyes are safe, even socially sanctioned, methods of being malicious. Simple to excuse if they're even noticed at all, and easy to hide, eye aggressions appear harmless." These tactics extend far beyond school-aged kids, with people using aggressive eye contact as a subtle form of bullying throughout life. "Employed to send warnings, set boundaries, punish, and establish dominance," Robinson writes, "aggressive eye contacts are used around the world to regulate behavior from a distance."

* *
* *

In *The Power of Eye Contact*, Ellsberg encourages his readers to "break your eye contact laterally, not vertically." The logic behind this advice? "Typically the lower-status individual in any interaction breaks eye contact first by looking down," Ellsberg explains. "This is as true in humans as in other primates. This is the classic 'look of shame.' It communicates 'You win; you're better than me; you have more power than me.'"

* *
* *

In Richard Chiem's lyric essay "Ten Times Gravity," he writes, "Eye contact is everything. Eye contact moves people to tears and calms them down like a magic potion. It means beauty, it means honesty, and it means respect." Chiem describes being physically abused by his mother as a child and how "during the beatings, she used to tell me to never look at her." He says now, as an adult: "My default is to look down and not giving you eye contact means you won't trust me. It means you think I'm timid, you think I'm rude, you think I'm not paying attention, you think I may be lying about something. You think I might be hiding something, like I have to prove I'm a real person."

* *
* *

In Ben Marcus's short story "The Dark Arts," the protagonist Julian travels to Düsseldorf to receive experimental treatments. Walking the streets, he feels on display in his sickly body. "Julian could only walk faster, wincing, until the shopkeepers released him from eye contact," Marcus writes. "Had anyone, he wondered, ever studied the biology of being seen? The ravaging, the way it literally burned when you fetched up in people's sight lines and they took aim at you with their minds?"

* *
* *

Author and autism advocate Joanna Grace writes, "Autistic people who use language to communicate have long spoken of how stressful eye contact is for them, with some even describing it as pain, burning and emotionally draining. Recently, scientists using MRI have been able to witness this pain in autistic brains. . . . Imagine if I asked you to hurt yourself and then asked you to do it again."

* *
* *

Once, at the bookstore, a customer brought a bag of books to sell, the titles entirely eye-contact related. As I looked through them, I felt just as odd and curious as I did with the fetish buys. The man had amassed a small collection of books whose purpose was all the same: to control others with one's eyes. Skimming through, I decided that they were all gross. I put my foot down; I wouldn't buy any. When he came up to check on his books, I handed him back the full bag and, with confidence, said, "We can't take any of these." He didn't say anything but held my gaze with a disarming force that made me question my decision. The power dynamic I'd anticipated had been flipped—even though I knew a secret about him, it turned out to be a secret he could use against me.

* *
* *

Remnants of my shyness aren't consistent, but appear suddenly, without warning. A group activity, a game at a party, an unexpected question I don't have the answer to—

something trips me up and I fall back into my old ways. I look down, study my feet, the ground, reminded once again of the embarrassment of being alive, the constant humiliation of being seen, of being in a body.

* *
* *

"Despite the frequent characterization of vision as atemporal and static, the eye can only do its job by being in almost constant motion," writes visual scholar Martin Jay. "Although it is, of course, possible to fix the gaze, we cannot really freeze movement of the eye for very long without incurring intolerable strain." What we interpret as eye contact's steady, unchanging state is really two pairs of eyes shifting, active, perpetually searching for new information.

* *
* *

Toward the end of Catron's four silent minutes of eye contact, having gotten past what she called "one of the more thrilling and terrifying experiences of my life," she began to see the eye as "not a window to anything but rather a clump of very useful cells. The sentiment associated with the eye fell away and I was struck by its astounding biological reality: the spherical nature of the eyeball, the visible musculature of the iris and the smooth wet glass of the cornea. It was strange and exquisite." Which makes me wonder: Do the physical details of the eyeball—the organ's squish and slime—contribute to the difficulty of eye contact? Perhaps the act of looking into another person's eyes reaches a point of discomfort when it reminds us how eyeballs are extensions of the brain, visible organs protruding through holes in the skull.

* *
* *

Rankine writes:

> In real life the looking away is the apology, despite the fact that when I look away I almost always feel guilty; I do not feel as if I have apologized. Instead I feel as if I have created a reason to apologize, I feel the guilt of having ignored that thing—the encounter. I could have nodded, I could have smiled without showing my teeth.

[TEN]

ONE OF THE STYLES OF LIVING

A CONVERSATION SERIES

This series uses only the words of the interview subjects, edited down from our longer recorded conversations.

KEITH ROSSON: novelist, short story author, former illustrator

"When I was doing illustration work, I didn't draw for fun. Ever. A lot of times a client would be like, 'I don't know what I want, so you should just come up with something,' and in that way I was drawing what I wanted. But when I had free time, I had zero interest in drawing.

"Given the severity of my tunnel vision—my lack of peripheral vision—I couldn't see the entire paper that I was working on all at once. So physically, there was a lot of rearing back to try to see the entire page. This also created a sort of two-dimensional flatness to my stuff. It could still be highly detailed, but life drawing and three-dimensional drawing were just tremendously hard for me, because essentially I couldn't see the whole object that I was drawing. I mean, I can't see the entire computer screen either, but that doesn't really matter when I'm writing.

"It got to the point where I was doing art and writing novels and short stories, and, just given the chaos of everything, the simplicity of writing started to appeal to me more and more—where it's just me and a screen. Versus doing stuff for bands, often for a record cover: I would need to get all of my paper, all of my art supplies, draw the stuff, run the sketches by the people, once they green-lit it I would have to scan it, then color it, and then run it by them again. After they approved that, I'd have to do all the layout; there were just constantly all these revisions and just so much *stuff*. Scanner, art supplies, stacks of paper, if you mess up on the paper it's hard to correct it on a black-and-white illustration in a way the client will be happy with. Before that, I was a painter. So, even more stuff—you have your canvases, tubes of paint, and brushes.

"I just got burnt on all of the accoutrements. The idea of me and a screen was just so appealing. So I started writing more and more and more. And the illustration stuff started to back away a little bit.

"For a long time, it had been my main source of income. But also, I'm legally blind and I was able to get disability. My partner always viewed it almost like a small monthly stipend to live a creative life. It's nowhere near enough to survive on—I didn't get anywhere near a thousand dollars a month—but it was so helpful. It gave me a lot of breathing room to use my free time to follow creative pursuits. But I had a lot of guilt about it for a long time. I guess it's just that capitalistic idea of not pulling your own weight or being a burden, socially. It took a lot of work to move past that mind state."

"I get the 'you don't look blind' thing a lot. I think it happens with all disabilities: There are degrees of disability, and it's hard for a lot of people to understand that. It's either you're in a wheelchair or you're not. You're either totally blind or you have twenty-twenty vision. It's hard for people to understand that disability is not a one-size-fits-all kind of thing. And with being an artist, people hear that or they see the work and are like, 'What do you mean you have a visual impairment? You made a picture.' It's not malicious, it's just a lack of knowledge.

"I grew up in a pretty intense household with a lot of addiction. And because my family was so entrenched in their own issues, I didn't find out I was visually impaired until I was ten or eleven. So, by the time I found out I was legally blind, I was already well-versed in art as an escape. And art as a joy. I was a voracious reader of comics books, copied comic books all the time, drew all the time.

"To her credit, when my mom got sober and discovered the depth of my impairment, she was never like, 'Oh, you can't do that; your eyes are too bad.' There was never any suggestion that I couldn't do art because of my disability.

"Before that, I just thought I was chubby and awkward. I had no clue that other people saw differently. Again, home was pretty intense, so I was pretty insular. I sought solace in stories and art. I had friends, but not to the point that people asked, 'What is *wrong* with this guy?' I was alone a lot of the time.

"I remember when I was around five, we had this upright sprinkler system—a big steel post—and I just ran right into it, full tilt. It took a divot out of my chest. Everyone just thought I was a clumsy kid. No one guessed that I ran into it because it was out of my field of vision."

"My entire life, I felt like I had such a scattershot approach creatively. I was always like, 'I'm a writer, I'm a painter, I'm an illustrator, I'm a graphic designer, I make zines,' but it felt like it all suffered because of that expansiveness. Now I feel like I'm honed in. I just write fiction. It feels way more rewarding. Doing all that other stuff was a lot of fun, but the scattered approach made each of those avenues not quite as good as they could have been.

"I got a two-book deal with Random House this year and sold the film option on the first. I'm currently writing the second book. To finally be, at forty-six years old, thrust into a career—one that's comfortable and fun—I just don't want to fuck it up. So I'm really trying to push forward."

[ELEVEN]

OFF-LABEL

IT HAPPENS WITH FACTORY-LIKE EFFICIENCY: a nurse numbs my eye with a series of drops, places an anesthetic-soaked sponge under my lower eyelid with tweezers, the doctor enters the room, shakes my hand, takes the sponge out, clamps my eye open. He tells me to look up, inserts a small needle, takes it out, unclamps my eye, shakes my hand again, and hurries off to inject another person's eyeball.

The drug in the needles is a colon-cancer medication called Avastin. It's used off-label to treat PXE and a number of conditions that affect the retina, the thin layer of light-sensitive tissue on the back of the eye. While the office's cold production-line efficiency doesn't make me feel especially important or cared for, it's understandable given the demand. The waiting room is never empty. Statistically speaking, most of the other patients are getting treated for the "wet" (a delicate way of saying "bloody") form of age-related macular degeneration, the leading cause of blindness in people over fifty. Some are probably getting treated for one of the common retinal afflictions among those with advanced-stage diabetes. There's a chance some are being treated for macular edema or retinal vein occlusion.

The odds are, that on any given day, I'm the only one there being treated for PXE. It's a condition rare enough that in a half-dozen ophthalmologists' offices over the years I've been made into a specimen—the whole office taking turns, looking at a type of retinal flaw they may never see again.

When I ask the nurse how many injections her office does every day, she has to think about it for a while, explaining that it varies since some people get both eyes while some only get one. "We have about thirty patients a day who get injections," she finally says.

"Do most people get used to them?"

She says it depends, but yeah, most people get used to them. I tell her that, even after all these years, I still can't get used to them.

"What don't you like about them?" she asks. From the outside, this is a ridiculous question: We're talking about injections into the eyeball. But her curiosity is sincere. Over the years, the procedure has become more streamlined—uncomfortable, but easy. I mention something about the soreness after, but I can't figure out how to tell a person who sees thirty people get injected every day, at least eleven thousand eyeball injections a year, how this simple procedure still shakes me, disrupting the core of my inner safety, triggering a brief depressive state I can't make sense of or name.

*

Even though my prescription is stronger than most, my glasses aren't noticeably thick. The whites of my eyes aren't prone to redness or discoloration, and my sky-blue irises tend to go unnoticed unless I wear a shirt of the same color. In my daily life, no one ever picks me out as a person with an eye condition. And since I tend not to mention it, it's likely that most of the people who know me don't realize the condition is something I deal with or think about every day.

No one knows exactly how rare PXE is because for some people it's a fairly quiet disease that often doesn't present problems until later in life, if at all. Since it's a genetic condition that affects tissue throughout the body, some people don't even struggle with the retinal aspect and instead suffer other bodily issues that don't point as easily to PXE as the root cause. Because of this, the incidence of the disease is only an estimate and, depending on who's estimating, can range from 1 in 100,000 people to 1 in 25,000. The room where I get injections has a wall of informational pamphlets about dozens of eye disorders, largely consisting of oddly named conditions I've never heard of—eyelid margin disease, cranial nerve palsy, optic neuritis, macular pucker—but nothing on PXE. It's apparently not yet considered common enough to justify having its own informational pamphlet. Perhaps this is a wise publishing decision; I've never met anyone else with the disease.

*

PXE creates a buildup of calcium in the elastic fibers of skin tissue and blood vessels. Aside from some bumpy necks or wrinkly elbows, the disease largely produces problems internally. Its presence in the retina doesn't cause blindness, it just creates the potential. Eye-wise, the main manifestation of the disease comes in the form of angioid streaks, permanent cracks in the area just behind the retina. The body can mistake one of these cracks as a hole it needs to patch up, growing a new blood vessel to heal the imagined wound. But these new vessels invariably hemorrhage, leaking blood and plasma, causing the whole structure of the retina to change, twisting and distorting one's perception of the world. If it happens in or near the macula, the part of the retina responsible for the central field of vision—which makes it possible to, among other things, recognize faces, read, and drive a car—it causes rapid vision loss and, if left untreated, blindness.

I suppose I'm lucky that my first hemorrhage happened when it did: If it had happened just a few years earlier, before the Avastin injections were widely available, I would have been getting the infamously ineffective cold laser treatments. Early on, in these waiting rooms, as a twentysomething receiving a treatment generally used for age-related conditions, I must have looked like a child to the other patients. I'm still typically the youngest one in the waiting room by at least a couple of decades.

Doctors aren't sure why some people with PXE experience hemorrhaging and some don't, why some have it earlier in life and some later, but they suspect eye trauma could be one reason (it's hard for me not to think back to one afternoon in my early twenties, when a friend of a friend accidentally jabbed his finger in my eye while we were playing basketball). Their only recommendations for PXE patients are to avoid heavy lifting and situations where the eyes are at risk. There are no preventative supplements or prescription drugs to take, only more injections—used preventatively, yet untested by patients or time.

So far, I've received nearly thirty injections—all in my right eye—and will likely continue to get injections for the rest of my life. How often I'll receive them, and how effective they'll be, is up for debate.

According to most online sources, Avastin's ophthalmological side effects read as "eye pain, subconjunctival hemorrhage (bloodshot eye), vitreous floaters, irregularity or swelling of the cornea, inflammation of the eye, and visual disturbances." The post-visit sheet I'm given each time I receive an injection explains that most of the side effects are due to the injection itself rather than the drug, with the most common being "burning sensation, bleeding on the outside of the eye, light sensitivity, blurred vision, air bubbles in your side vision and bloody tears." I'm told not to worry if bloody tears occur, though that seems impossible.

Avastin was designed to cut off oxygen to cancer cells in hopes of quelling vessel growth in tumors, receiving FDA approval to treat colon cancer in 2004. This made it the first drug on the market to inhibit vessel growth, and ophthalmologists had been waiting for a drug that did exactly that. Almost immediately, some of them began trying it out on patients with serious retinal conditions and reporting its clinical effectiveness. Within a few years, Avastin injections replaced laser treatments as the most common procedure for dealing with retinal issues.

Even with the 2006 arrival of the FDA-approved, designed-for-retinal-use drug Lucentis, off-label Avastin use continued. Lucentis is manufactured by Genentech, the same company that produces Avastin, and Lucentis was meant to replace the off-label use of Avastin entirely. Lucentis is closely related to the Avastin antibody but made up of slightly smaller molecules that theoretically should be more effective for use in the eye. But according to numerous studies, the two drugs have "virtually the same efficacy."

The difference is price. Genentech prefers doctors to use the $2,000-a-dose Lucentis over the now $50-a-dose Avastin, but patients will usually risk off-label use in the interest of saving a couple thousand dollars. Many low-income patients, myself included, are never even presented with the option to choose Lucentis. In terms of production and chemistry, there seems to be no clear reason for the price difference.

Genentech has threatened to block Avastin distribution to pharmacies that repackage the drug into doses suitable for the eye. According to a *New York Times* report, the company has offered "secret rebates" to some ophthalmologists to convince them to switch over to the pricier Lucentis.

When I email Genentech to see if they have plans to someday seek FDA approval for the ophthalmological use of Avastin, they write back saying they are "unable to address [the] request without verbal discussion." So I call and they pass me around to several different departments before a nervous chemist tells me what I've already assumed: no plans to seek FDA approval, just a continued focus on marketing

Lucentis. Which means that research on Avastin will continue to be limited, and the drug will remain a wild card for thousands of people around the world.

After treatment, there's a small red circle in the lower right corner of my eye where the needle went in. Often, depending on how the treatment goes, the entire white of the eye is red and irritated. Lighter colored eyes dilate more and stay dilated longer than darker colored eyes, so my right pupil becomes particularly enormous, overtaking the iris, and staying like this for seven or eight hours. Sunglasses have always disoriented me, so unless it's an exceptionally bright day, I show my eye to the world. It makes fellow train commuters cautious. Dilated eyes can signal a state of psychosis, or the ingestion of hallucinogenic drugs, and the single dilated eye signals, at best, a potentially unhealthy obsession with David Bowie.

On my way home from today's injection, I observe the conversation of the teens across from me slowly quieting as they each take notice of the guy with the one giant pupil facing them. The state of my eye isn't quite recognizable enough to be funny, nor horrific enough to be gross, so they just quietly steal glances. Meanwhile, I'm experiencing floaters—specks of gelatinous inner-eye material—bouncing around my field of vision, keeping me in a constant state of distraction. My eye will stay dried out and sore for the rest of the day, with some residual ache tomorrow.

During the time I've been receiving Avastin treatments, the injections have gone from being expensive and dramatic to relatively brief and affordable procedures. Today, an injection is a small dose of Avastin given with a small needle—a quick poke in the eye. It's like someone aggressively putting in a contact lens for you. When I first started receiving the treatments, getting an Avastin injection was a more involved process. Doctors weren't yet sure how to adjust the dosage for use in the eye, so they used larger doses, injected with a larger gauge of needle. They treated it more like a surgery, assembling a team of nurses to be on hand—each step, including the injection itself, was long and drawn out.

Despite the comparative ease of the injections these days, what hasn't changed is how I feel afterward. No matter how much I prepare myself, the undirected, unnamable sadness always takes me by surprise.

For years, my doctor has been trying to get me on the Avastin schedule. It would be easier for him if I were like most of his other patients. If I just went along with the office's factory-like system and received a shot every four to six weeks. The fact that I'm hesitant to follow a protocol established for patients twice my age, hesitant to give in to a lifetime of monthly eyeball injections, is frustrating and somewhat puzzling to him.

His argument is hard to dismiss: A regular injection program is preventative care. The retina suffers permanent damage when a person waits until hemorrhaging occurs to get injections, as I've been doing, and regular injections keep rogue blood vessels from growing in the first place. Avastin has a high success rate in ophthalmological use and its immediate side effects are generally manageable.

To him, my concern is too hypothetical, just a *what if.* But I can't be the only one who thinks regularly injecting a colon cancer drug into an eyeball could prove to be a bad idea. What if the cumulative long-term effects are worse than the slight post-hemorrhage damage, or worse than being blind? History is full of well-intentioned preventative measures backfiring. Every time I get an injection, I can't help but imagine it one day becoming part of a preventative-failure montage, playing alongside video clips of children getting sprayed down with DDT.

Few research papers or doctors acknowledge the mysteries of long-term use—nearly all of them are solely concerned with the treatment's immediate effectiveness. The most direct acknowledgment I've found is a line slipped into a summary of an Avastin-Lucentis comparative study: "The small benefits of receiving monthly treatments might not outweigh the medical risks of having the treatment so often."

Frequently, I feel ungrateful—still being so skeptical about a treatment that's saved my vision so many times. But it's not a lack of gratitude so much as a lack of faith in medical science; no matter how much I may benefit, I don't fully trust it.

If I follow my doctor's advice, and begin receiving injections every four to six weeks, I will receive over five hundred eye injections in my lifetime (assuming I live an average lifespan). Some of his patients have received over one hundred, but given Avastin's brief existence, few have received more than that. And given the age of most patients, the majority of these people—unless they live well into the triple digits—will pass away before making it to two hundred injections, let alone five hundred. So, while they may have other concerns I don't have, they probably don't worry about the long-term side effects of Avastin.

No one really knows what Avastin injections will do over time, so if there's a catch—a tolerance issue, a serious adverse effect from years of use—I'll be the first to find out.

After I get home, I hole myself away in my basement room, away from my roommates. I watch movies alone, timing my trips to the bathroom or kitchen by the sounds coming from upstairs so I won't have to talk to anyone, turning into a timid, fearful version of myself that I like to believe I aged out of in my early twenties. I don't understand the reaction, but I often imagine it as something primal, something base—a survival response to having a stranger take a sharp instrument to a crucial sensory organ. There's a reason so many people are squeamish about having their eyes touched, a reason why eye prodding, poking, and cutting are used in film to shock and disturb: Being poked in the eye is a strange violation.

[TWELVE]

BETTE DAVIS EYES

A BRIEF HISTORY

(THERE THEY ARE, STEALING THE SHOW from the rest of her body: Wide in perpetual surprise, full of righteous indignation. Narrowing, muscles tensing, then relaxing, hinting at an understanding reached, a plan for revenge coursing down into her limbs. Bette Davis's eyes, the eyes that became famous: lake-water blue, appearing hazel on black-and-white film. Lids slowly bobbing, lashes long, pupils giant, eyeballs overcoming their sockets, seemingly ready to leave the skull.)

Growing up with my grandparents, I watched more black-and-white movies from their generation than I did color films from mine. I didn't know who Molly Ringwald or John Cusack were, but I knew Katharine Hepburn and Jimmy Stewart well. I recited Marx Brothers' lines by heart and imitated Charlie Chaplin's walk. But the image I associated most strongly with the era of movies we often watched was Bette Davis.

As far as I was concerned, her movies weren't particularly memorable or interesting. They tended to blend together in my mind, but Davis herself stuck out. She was simply *different*. She confused my categorical understanding of the world. She had a way of looking both youthful and ancient, grotesque and glamorous, and her characters were often mean-spirited antiheroines. She was the evil twin, the cruel matriarch, the woman who stole her sister's husband, the nanny who drowned the baby. She was the sex worker threatening the gangster, "I'll get you if I have to come back from the grave to do it." The woman telling her sickly husband, "I hope you die. I hope you die soon. I'll be waiting for you to die."

According to one of her biographers, Ed Sikov, "Few have equaled Davis's capacity to risk generating an audience's thoroughgoing contempt, let alone openly invite it. . . . She dares us to hate her, and we often do."

(In her first film, 1931's *Bad Sister*, twenty-three-year-old Davis, a rail in a flapper dress, an Olive Oyl look-alike, stares up at the man she admires as if she's under hypnosis—or, more likely, attempting to hypnotize him. Each time her heavy lids open, it's almost shocking.)

*

Thirty years after her death and nearly eighty years since the height of her fame, Davis remains fixed in our cultural memory. There are over a dozen biographies recounting the bottomless drama of her personal and professional lives, all while trying to crack the mystery beneath Davis's hard exterior.

Her combination of over-the-top delivery, cool demeanor, and unapologetic vitriol have made her a favorite of drag performers for generations. Her lifelong feud with Joan Crawford is one of old Hollywood's most-told stories, a battle grand enough to fill up a five-hundred-page book and inspire a high-budget, star-studded 2017 television series. Few stars from her era have any kind of name recognition today, and yet, even as most of her films sink out of favor, Davis continues to glare at us, living on in her infamy.

(Her eyes, in her 1934 breakthrough, *Of Human Bondage*, paving the path for the roles she would become most known for. After perhaps the defining glamorous Golden Age close-up—giant eyes, soft-focused over a glass of champagne—her character sinks into disrepute. Flooded in eyeliner, donning a lace slip, fake pearl necklace, thick black belt riding high over a velvet coat, she looks decades ahead of her time: heroin chic, pre-punk. The eyes sell the depravity. Under their made-up layers there's a hardness, a meanness, a true dissatisfaction impossible to fake.)

*

According to Davis, it was only because of her eyes that her first three-month contract was renewed. After her screen test, Universal Studios head Carl Laemmle Jr. had this to say: "She has about as much sex appeal as [gangly character actor] Slim Summerville."

Director Michael Curtiz described her as a "goddamned nothing no good sexless son of a bitch." According to Davis, he also referred to her as "the unsexiest woman I have ever seen in my life."

From the beginning, her looks were remarked upon, openly debated, even in the midst of praise. Novelist Graham Greene observed "pale ash-blonde hair, the popping neurotic eyes, a kind of corrupt and phosphorescent prettiness."

Warner Bros. studio head Jack Warner noted a "magic quality that transformed this sometimes bland and not beautiful little girl into a great artist."

The well of insults and backhanded compliments aimed at Davis's physical appearance runs deep. From our vantage point, it's easy to see the level of objectification, the misogyny, the constricting limitations placed upon her. But biographers still do it today; I'm doing it right now: defining this woman by her body.

We generally feel more comfortable doing this with the eyes, though, because we're talking about body parts we don't consider private. They're just out there on display, doing their job. Not only are the eyes public, we believe they hold secrets, answers. *The windows to the soul*, we say. It's not objectification, we tell ourselves, but a way of understanding.

Eyes reveal, to some degree, how a person is feeling in a particular moment, and it takes a good actor or liar or sociopath (all of which Davis has been called) to fully hide it. Some looked into Davis's eyes and saw beauty or sex. Some saw ugliness, disdain, even some form of evil. But so much of what we see in a pair of eyes is just ourselves, projected onto another, then peering back.

"Hollywood always wanted me to be pretty," said Davis, "but I fought for realism."

(In *The Letter*, she shoots the man she loves, putting bullets in him long after he's dead, her eyes shining in the moonlight, their vast expanse revealing a mixture of horror and satisfaction. Just six years after her breakthrough, at only thirty-two, she looks as if she's aged a couple decades—her character a curious combo of noir femme fatale and quaint grandmother. In the lie her character tells of the shooting, the man's unwanted advances began with him saying, "You have very pretty eyes.")

It was on an airplane fifteen years ago that I first grappled with the notion that Bette Davis might be more than an image, more than a Mid-Atlantic accent or a symbol of movie nights at my grandparents' house. My friend and I were seated next to a middle-aged British man who was charmed by us barely twentysomething oddballs. At some point, I asked him about the book lying facedown on his lap. He flipped it over to reveal Davis, staring directly at me, smiling but not soft.

The man told us how, in his reading, he looked past her personal dramas to see her solely as a force who changed history—a woman who took on the male-dominated power structures of Hollywood from a young age and never stopped pushing to get what she wanted. She was the Golden Age starlet who talked back, who fought—and even sued—for equal pay, better roles, more complex female characters, who was never satisfied and famously "got most of her exercise by putting her foot down."

Our seatmate's passion for her was palpable, and when I got home, I decided to start watching Bette Davis's films intentionally to try to see what they revealed. But what I found there was another layer: a secret—or the suggestion of a secret—buried in her eyes that was hard to define but kept me watching.

(In *All About Eve*, it's the lids: those oft-ignored flaps of skin, constantly spreading tears across the surface of the eye, warding off invasion, blocking the light out during sleep. Davis's lids hang so low, their weight so palpable, they almost appear to be a biological anomaly. In *Eve*, the lids shield her eyeballs as they move about with a mind of their own, like two twitching cat tails, moving in unison. The half-mast lids are her character's trick, sending off a signal of inattentiveness, creating an illusion of intoxication or exhaustion, while she covertly scans the room, her gaze filled with purpose.)

What we see in other people's eyes is often not the result of emotional depth but rather evidence of the body's interior health. Through the eyeballs, we can see signs of alcohol and drug abuse, allergies, infections, high cholesterol, certain types of cancer, stress, sleep issues, and a host of other diseases and conditions.

These days, some suggest that Davis's unusual eyes were a consequence of Graves' disease, an autoimmune thyroid condition. Swelling the muscles and surrounding tissues around the eyes, the condition pushes the eyeballs forward, limiting their movement and causing them to protrude. This is pure internet-age speculation, and it's perhaps unlikely that someone with Davis's level of wealth and access to medical professionals would have had a serious disease slip by undiagnosed. Still, I can't help but wonder: When are eyes windows to the soul and when are they windows to the body? How often do we look into a pair of eyes and misinterpret health—or illness—for emotion?

(Her eyes, in *Whatever Happened to Baby Jane?*: radiant, satisfied as she kicks her sister across the floor. In *Hush . . . Hush Sweet Charlotte*: soaking up a lightning storm, leaning over the rail of a balcony, the wind in her hair, wild-eyed. Looking to the ground, lids heavy, having struck down her enemies once again.)

It's *Baby Jane* and *Sweet Charlotte* that are, perhaps deservedly, the most remembered and discussed Davis films today. They exhibit her at her wildest, her most unhinged, and are backed by scripts that do her talents justice. But they also initiated the so-called "hagsploitation" subgenre: aging actresses portraying formerly glamorous women who are now struggling with their mental health, threatening the lives and well-being of those around them. These types of characterizations are at once commentaries on how aging women are disregarded by our culture, while also fully embracing the belief that older women are not only unattractive but horrifying—roles Davis thrived in while also being ashamed of. But, like many of her earlier performances, they set a new precedent; their existence and popularity brought opportunities for more complex roles.

"Just watching Bette Davis on the screen was empowering to women," says Jane Fonda. "It's like: this is what's possible; this is the range and depth that is possible for a woman."

Meryl Streep adds: "Bette Davis seemed willing, she even had an appetite, for parts that were conventionally unappealing. She changed the requirement that actresses in the movies invariably be likable or attractive. She lifted the veil of appropriate behavior in women to expose what was scary, unexpected, or ugly . . . Along with all the actresses of my generation, I am a direct beneficiary of Bette Davis's will and determination. Because of her hard-fought achievements, we all had it a little easier."

(Her eyes, in *The Nanny*: bulging under thickly painted eyebrows, over deeply lined bags, eyelids blinking quickly. Ostensibly in a role of servitude, but clearly holding the power.)

Davis begins her 1962 autobiography, *The Lonely Life*, with these words: "I have always been driven by some distant music—a battle hymn no doubt—for I have been at war from the beginning." Is this what we see when we look into her eyes? Beyond the unlikely result of genetics and her skill as an actress, do we see the lonely starlet, at war with the world, the self perpetually bursting through the role she's playing?

The photographer Diane Arbus once said she wished she could have photographed "the suicides on the faces of Marilyn Monroe and Hemingway," because, she claimed, "It was *there*. Suicide was *there*." Though Davis didn't kill herself, her daughter claims her mother staged suicide attempts to punish her children, and Davis's assorted struggles with mental health are well documented. But even those closest to her often didn't understand what was behind her struggles.

"She was not a 'safe' person to have around," says producer William Frye. "She was capable of blowing up at any moment."

"Her unhappiness seeped through to the rest of us," James Cagney laments.

"Davis was an angry woman for reasons nobody who knew her ever adequately explained to me and for reasons I still cannot fully understand," writes Sikov in his Davis biography.

Was that sadness and anger there: on her face, in her eyes? When I watch her films, I sometimes imagine I'm seeing a depression too grand to look away from.

(In *The Anniversary*, her left eye covered with a curiously quarter-note-shaped eye patch, looking stylish enough to kick off a future film trope. The right eye so alive, so active. Shimmering. Cheery, almost, as she rips each member of her family, and prospective member of her family, down, one by one.)

Friends ask what draws me in, fascinated with my fascination, and I tell them, to their dissatisfaction: I'm curious about everyone else's curiosity. They ask what I see in her eyes, and I have no answer. How do you separate the person from the character the actor is playing? At best, I'm looking for the real Davis in the cracks of the roles she was cast in. But with her entire adult life lived in the spotlight, when was she not playing a role? As she writes, "It has been my experience that one cannot, in any shape or form, depend on human relations for any lasting reward. It is only work that truly satisfies." So perhaps the work is the best place to understand her, the place to meet her where she preferred to be met.

"She had," writes Sikov, "more than any performer I have ever studied, a blazing ability to imprint herself onto every character she ever played—to make me believe in those fictive characters while never letting me forget that I was watching *her*, a calculating actress, an intuitive star. Bette Davis forces audiences to notice her as Bette Davis even when she is most deeply immersed in her roles."

I don't know her secrets, my life and world are nothing like hers, but I like the possibilities her famed eyes present: a windows-of-the-soul Rorschach test spanning nearly a century of pop culture. What does each person see? What does it say about us that we've been staring so hard, caring so much, for so long?

*

(Her eyes, in her final film, *Wicked Stepmother*: lackadaisical, often bordering on closed, an intentional lethargy, bored by the terrible script, the awful cast surrounding her, her eyes doing more work than anyone on set.)

It's through Kim Carnes's "Bette Davis Eyes"—the biggest hit of 1981 and still a staple of twenty-four-hour grocery stores—that we have an anthem for Davis's lasting ocular mystique. "She's got Bette Davis eyes," Carnes croons, her voice filled with apparent passion and meaning, but saying almost nothing. Broadly, it's a song in the "Maneater" vein—a woman who seduces for sport—but to listeners unaware of who Bette Davis is, there are few lyrical clues to what these eyes actually look like. There's no mention of their size, their color, their life—if, truly like Davis's, they seem to lead an existence separate from the woman herself. In the song, Davis's eyes are just a stand-in, a phrase that asks each listener to summon up their own idea of what "Bette Davis eyes" might signify. The anthemic chorus reminding us, again and again, of the meaning we make out of pressurized, gel-filled spheres. Reminding us that eyes not only see but are seen.

[THIRTEEN]

THE NOBLEST OF THE SENSES

A CATALOG

1.

IN A WORLD FULL OF ILLUSIONS AND MIRAGES, photoshopped images and deepfakes, blind spots and substance-induced hallucinations, sighted people still believe they know the truth when they see it. Even after decades of research into the unreliability of eyewitness testimony, their faith in their own eyes remains strong. It's always different when it's personal, when the eyewitness is you. When it's your own eyes, it's difficult for the mind to let go of the thing you have seen, or the thing you think you have seen. *I saw it with my own eyes*, we say. And with that, we have all the proof we need.

2.

René Descartes famously called sight the "noblest" of the senses, adding, "The inventions which serve to augment its power are among the most useful that there can be." Today it seems ridiculous to think of the senses in terms of virtue or social class. And yet, the lofty status of sight is truer now than when Descartes wrote the words in 1637, just as the printing press was shouldering aside oral traditions. In the centuries since, inventors have hewed closely to the philosopher's advice: consider everything from film cameras to televisions, computers to smartphones, emojis taking the place of words.

We live in an ocularcentric culture—one that prioritizes sight over all other senses—and as technology moves forward, adding screen upon screen, vision's reign spreads. It's the sense we give the bulk of our responsibilities to and work the hardest to please. Sight has, in effect, moved up the social ladder from nobility to royalty.

"The fundamental event of the modern age is the conquest of the world as picture," philosopher Martin Heidegger says. Because of this conquest, and the length of its rule, we're no longer fully aware to what degree we rely on vision, or that there's anything lost in relying on one sense so completely. "The predominance of sight is so deeply embedded," writes political theorist Hannah Arendt, "that we seldom find any consideration bestowed on it, as though it belonged among things too obvious to be noticed."

3.

"The eyes are hungry," W. A. Mathieu writes in *The Listening Book*. "They eat brain energy. When you close your eyes your brain opens to your ears; sound rushes in to fill the sphere of the skull." When I was in my early twenties, I read Mathieu's books about the hidden music of daily life, hoping to train my ears, to hear the world differently, to open myself to experience in a way I didn't yet know how to do.

Popular with aging hippies, the books weren't cool, weren't something I shared with my roommates and friends, but, when no one was around, I tried out Mathieu's often ridiculous exercises. Humming along with the refrigerator's motor. Harmonizing with the phone's dial tone. Testing the resonance of objects by drumming on them. Uttering sounds and syllables to remember the joy of language.

Mostly I felt foolish. But every now and then, I let my guard down enough to have fun, to be a child, to discover. I closed my eyes, wrapping myself in a wool blanket and curling up in front of the stereo speakers, trying to forget what I looked like while I assigned textures to tones. "Open your eyes," Mathieu instructs, "now the brain is crowded, and the bright screen of sound grows dim." And it was always true: the visual world had a way of narrowing what the ear could take in, of turning the volume down.

Around this time, a friend introduced me to walking meditation, or at least a drastically simplified version she learned in a class on mindfulness. "Just close your eyes," she told me as we walked down the street. After a few steps, we bumped into each other and stopped, laughing. But the next day, while I was walking alone in the woods, I reached a stretch of wide, well-maintained path. I closed my eyes and felt the forces of the world rush toward me. It wasn't just that my brain opened to my ears, but that my whole body opened to the wind, the small plants under my feet, the trees that towered over the path. My moderate pace suddenly felt wild and reckless. There was no way, it seemed, to know what I was walking into, my peaceful stroll now so full of risk.

4.

Philosopher David Michael Kleinberg-Levin writes, "There is a very strong tendency in vision to grasp and fixate . . . a tendency to dominate, secure, and control." Levin describes "the specters of patriarchal rule" that haunt our ocularcentric culture—vision's aggressive desire to possess—a desire that can be directed toward a person, groups of people, and entire cultures.

One could argue that our fixation on vision is the source of most of the great injustices and cruelties across history. But there's a slippery slope in damning vision entirely, when perhaps it's due more to the importance we place on it—the drunk power of vision's nobility. What gets lost when we dull the other senses in favor of a single sense? How does being disconnected from our bodies change how we exist in the world and how we judge other bodies?

5.

"The eyes want to collaborate with the other senses," says architect Juhani Pallasmaa. The senses aren't meant to take turns—to see something, then touch it, then smell it, then listen to it—but to work in concert. In the words of ancient philosopher Xenophanes, "It is the whole that sees, the whole that thinks, the whole that hears."

These days, with images coming in faster than ever and arriving through largely passive interactions, our senses don't have a chance to collaborate. "The only sense that is fast enough to keep pace with the astounding increase of speed in the technological world is sight," observes Pallasmaa. Consequently, it's only when our vision is in some way limited that our other senses come alive. We feel our way through the dark, aware of the slightest change in the air, listening.

[FOURTEEN]

ONE OF THE STYLES OF LIVING

A CONVERSATION SERIES

This series uses only the words of the interview subjects, edited down from our longer recorded conversations.

ANDREW LELAND: writer, podcaster, former editor at the *Believer* magazine, author of the memoir *The Country of the Blind*

"The whole time I was at the *Believer* I didn't write a lot—I did a book review for the *Chronicle* and I had this freaky blog that was just nonsense—basically just a language nozzle. I always felt guilt that I was in this little privileged literary position and I wasn't taking advantage of it by being one of those intellectuals who can run the day-to-day operations of a monthly magazine and also publish three-thousand-word review essays in the *Nation* or whatever. But I just didn't have the bandwidth to do that at all. I remember I would just write these little pieces and, as I did, I noticed that pretty much all of them had hints of stuff about blindness.

"Like, there was a newspaper issue of *McSweeney's* that was like a Sunday *New York Times* from an alternate universe, and I wrote a letter to the editor that was about what I would miss about punctuation on the page. It was just two paragraphs long, but it's funny for me to think back on that and think that when I finally decided to write more seriously—in a way where I wasn't forcing myself to write a book review because I thought I should, or language-nozzle nonsense—blindness was there. Even though at that time I didn't own a cane, I think I still drove during the day—actually, I know I did—so blindness was a very distant feeling. But it was still there. I had the diagnosis, and I knew that things were changing.

"There was a reading series that asked me to give a talk, and I did this more involved piece about blindness and art. Then I ended up adapting that for *McSweeney's*, and it ran as an essay. That talk and essay felt like a coming out. That was about six years ago now. And I think the biggest difference was that I was using a cane just about everywhere I went. At that time, I don't think I was using much assisted tech for reading, but definitely for mobility I was, and I hadn't driven for about five or six years at that point. I'd stopped riding a bike. So I definitely felt like I was at—not a crossroads, but an inflection point of some kind, where it felt like there was more urgency to write about it.

"It's a weirdly unpoetic story of how it actually became a book project. There was the larger thing of just knowing I wanted to write a book, and, as I wrote more and more about blindness, it just seemed clear that that would make sense in some very vague way. But at that time in my life, I was very involved in audio work, and I originally conceived of it as a multipart audio project. I saw a call for proposals, so proposed this series, they accepted it, and that led to interest from a podcast company. So I got pretty far into developing it as a podcast series, and then that imploded. Just for capitalistic reasons, or whatever you want to call it—'media business reasons.' But I also think it in part imploded because I was secretly not into the way it was going. Even though I felt a professional obligation to ride that wave, it was a bad wave. So it imploded and I was disappointed but also secretly relieved.

"Very luckily, that process of implosion landed me with a literary agent, and she was like, 'Yeah dude, this is a book.' And I was like, 'Oh, right. I knew that.' I wish it had more of that poetic 'then I just went into my attic and told everyone to go away because I had to do it.' There were elements of the process that were definitely like that, but it almost felt like I got a job, and the job was to write this book. And it was an amazing job, but I had to summon the inner resources to do it.

"But part of it is just pleasure. I love that feeling of discovery. That's one cliché I definitely get behind: learning what you know by writing. In the same way that I was confounded by whether to be offended or delighted by a TV show that cast a sighted actress in a blind role and felt the need to write about it, there was this much larger confusion and curiosity and fear—just a totally uncanny cocktail of feelings—around my vision loss. Figuring out how I feel about my own relationship with my vision loss, or with my blindness, or with the vision that I still have, was definitely hugely refined and articulated and explored. I'm not done, but I'm done with the book."

[FIFTEEN]

DRY EYES

I SET UP ON THE FLOOR OF THE TRAILER I SHARED with my mom, baseball cards spread out in front of me, ready for game six of the World Series. My favorite team, Atlanta, was playing Toronto. I loved Atlanta because of their precise pitchers who created slow-paced games with more strikeouts than hits. It wasn't the kind of baseball a ten-year-old was supposed to like, but I was a pitcher in Little League, and my dream was to someday pitch no-hitters. I didn't throw particularly fast or use a lot of clever changeups, but I was careful, consistent, better than my teammates at not letting my emotions get the best of me.

The game went into extra innings, and I was transfixed by the low score, the held tension. When Toronto scored two runs in the top of the eleventh, I got nervous. In the bottom of the inning, Atlanta looked like they were going to tie it, even win it.

But they fell short.

There, in the woods of rural Washington, as far from the game as possible while still being in the continental United States, I wept. I rarely cried, rarely felt the need to cry, but baseball was my life, and the World Series was the most important event I could imagine. Atlanta losing meant that I had to wait a year to see them try again, and a year was a lifetime. By myself, on the floor, my tears went on and on; I couldn't make them stop.

Last year I didn't cry. Or at least I can't think of a single time during that twelve-month stretch when tears actually made it out of my eyes and onto my cheeks. I'm not sure whether I've developed a block around tears or just a block around the memory of tears. Perhaps this wouldn't interest me so much if I hadn't spent the bulk of my adulthood preoccupied with my emotional health, dissecting my reactions to life's various challenges for clues explaining why I am the way I am, believing myself to be emotionally aware.

I cried when two of my friends died in a warehouse fire a little over a year ago. I cried a few months before that when my cousin died from a blood clot that formed in the middle of the night—weeks after a leg amputation that had gone well. I cried when one of my closest friends intentionally jumped from the top of a waterfall to his death a year-and-a-half prior, and when an old high school friend shot himself a couple years before that.

But each time, I didn't cry much, and only with one other person, never in public, or even in private. At each of their respective funerals or memorials, my eyes welled up, but tears didn't leave my eyes. This was never due to any conscious stifling, nor tangible shame or remnants of shame around crying in public, but just because my body didn't feel the need to weep.

I talk to each of these lost loved ones on occasion; I write letters to them, I think of things I need to tell them, books and albums I want to recommend, I laugh at our inside jokes and think about how these jokes are only inside of me now. Sometimes their absence hits me in the grocery store or on the bus, the pressure filling my chest, and I wonder if I can handle its force—if I'm built to love as many people as I do since love also means so much heartbreak, so much loss.

I call my best friend and ask her, "How much have you seen me cry?" Aside from a handful of memorable moments of sadness in our seventeen-year relationship, she tells me that most of her memories of me crying involve me laughing. And it's true: I used to laugh to the point of tears on a fairly regular basis. But I can't even remember doing that last year. And her reminder that I cry from laughter doesn't alleviate my worry that I'm blocked emotionally. That somehow, I have forgotten how to cry in sadness, in heartache, in grief.

During the era I obsessed over slow baseball games, I listened almost exclusively to the oldies station. At the time, "oldies" meant music from when the term rock 'n' roll was coined in 1951 to somewhere around the Summer of Love. While I've never heard anyone refer to this period as the golden age of crying songs, a case could easily be made for it.

The station played "Lonely Teardrops," "96 Tears," "Valley of Tears," "Letter Full of Tears," "Tears of a Clown,"

"Drown in My Own Tears," and "The Tracks of My Tears." They played "Cry," "Cry Baby," "Cry Like a Baby," "It's Time to Cry," "I'm Gonna Sit Right Down and Cry (Over You)," "(If You Cry) True Love, True Love," "Big Girls Don't Cry," "Judy's Turn to Cry," "Cry to Me," and I loved them all.

Perhaps more than any other song, though, I loved Roy Orbison's "Crying," which remains one of the most commonly referenced songs about crying more than a half-century after its release. "I was alright," Orbison begins, "for a while." Gradually, he unveils how far from alright he's fallen, and by the end of the song's compact two minutes and forty-five seconds, he's breaking down, the star of his own tragic opera. It's nearly impossible to listen to his lack of restraint, his unapologetic sincerity, without having some kind of reaction—it's either deeply moving or hilariously over the top, and not much in between. As a kid, the song's haunting passion enchanted me. It didn't seem disturbed. I understood that this is what people did: they cried over other people. This level of passion was natural and right. Even if I didn't always show it, I felt it.

Science separates tears into three categories: the continuous tears that moisturize our eyes, the reflex tears that appear when we yawn and that flush out fallen eyelashes, and the emotional tears we release when we are in some way moved. These categories are broad. It seems silly to include the tears from being punched in the face in the same category as the tears from chopping an onion. And even worse—fundamentally wrong, even—to lump the tears that come from watching a loved one succeed together with the tears that come from watching a loved one die. The range of emotional tears, especially, is so great that it seems each deserves its own category, its own word, its own bit of recognition.

As far as we know, humans are the only species to produce tears of emotion. Charles Darwin called emotional tears one of the "special expressions of man." Literary critic Tom Lutz deems the act of crying to be a "human universal," since "[t]hroughout history, and in every culture, emotional tears are shed—everyone, everywhere, cries at some time."

Yet, despite their ubiquity, no one really understands why we cry tears of emotion. Some have conceived of tears as just a biological overflow of unwanted toxins. Some have pointed to the painkilling neurotransmitter unique to emotional tears and have suggested we cry because doing so offers a pleasurable chemical hit. And across the ages, many have considered tears a cathartic emotional necessity. While most of our current cultural attitude around emotional tears treats the idea of catharsis as a basic truth, even that's up for debate. "After a century of therapeutic theorizing and research, there is still no hard evidence that tears are in fact cathartic," Lutz writes in *Crying: The Natural & Cultural History of Tears*, "and there is some to suggest that they are not."

Obscuring this "human universal" even further is the fact that the norms around crying differ wildly between cultures, and, as much as we've been led to believe otherwise, gendered attitudes around tears have no consistency through history or across cultures. I worry my block is due to an aspect of male socialization I have yet to kick. Perhaps I'm unconsciously idealizing an image of an unemotional stoicism that was pushed on me by the larger culture, even as I've spent years critiquing it, making fun of it, thinking I was past it.

In the absence of my biological father, the men in my early life were my grandpa and my uncle, two caring and emotionally open men. Though neither cried a lot, it wasn't unusual to see them cry, and they never told me it was something to be ashamed of. I've often felt like I lucked out, getting to grow up around them. But the culture as a whole—from characters in movies to the men in our small town—convinced me men should be ashamed to cry.

My childhood could accurately be depicted as a montage of my emotional friends being told to suck it up by their angry dads. At school, kids who cried were made fun of, becoming targets for bullies. So I got good at holding it in. I know some of this instinct to suppress my tears has stuck around, but I have no idea how to identify where it begins or ends. How do we make a distinction between socialization and honest emotional reaction? Time weaves them together, making them appear one and the same.

Several years ago, I had the flu, a fever that made me weak, leaving me stuck on a basement futon, watching movie after movie. During this marathon, I put on *Footloose*, a movie I'd always mocked for its seemingly improbable town-that-bans-dancing plot. But in my sickness and desire to be entertained, I cast all doubts aside. By the time Kevin Bacon—as outsider, dance-obsessed bad kid Ren McCormack—stepped to the front of the town-hall meeting, I was invested. He quoted Bible passages that portrayed dancing not as the sinful activity the town council insisted it was, but as a celebration of God, the natural reaction to religious ecstasy, turning the town's ideology back on itself. Lying in bed, covered in layers of blankets, cold and alone, I wept. This speech, I felt, righted a great injustice, conveying a depth that was obscured by the movie's surface. I was a mess.

The scene changed. John Lithgow—as record-burning, anti-dance activist Reverend Shaw Moore—rehearsed his sermon in front of empty pews, his wild daughter watching from the back, and I kept right on crying.

Later, when my roommates got home from work and asked how I was doing, I told them I had bawled to *Footloose*, and we all laughed, amused that my weak state of mind made me cry to a film whose most memorable scene involves two tractors playing chicken. But after my fever passed, I rewatched it, and cried again.

This is what confuses me most as I sift through my memories of tears, dredging up some of these smaller, less-obvious episodes: they're rarely based on the degree of emotion I feel, or feel I should feel.

Maybe the inconsistency of tears is just one of their universal mysteries, but it seems most people can say they always cry in response to specific situations, and I just can't. I've sat dry-eyed at dozens of weddings and funerals while everyone around me wept, but I once cried while donating a car that had been sitting in my driveway for months. I don't cry following large-scale tragedies where I don't know any of the deceased, even though I've lost friends and acquaintances to mass shootings and catastrophic fires. I've never cried when any of my favorite musicians, writers, or actors have died, but I've cried multiple times while getting garden beds ready for winter. I can't put any of the memories together and make sense of them.

Last year was the worst year for American politics in my lifetime. There were upheavals and fallouts in my family. I dealt with multiple health issues. I produced some of the most vulnerable pieces of writing I've ever worked on. It should have been a year for crying.

My friends regularly tell me about how a good cry can help them get through a tough situation. I wish I had that kind of relationship with crying. It's hard for me to call my current relationship with crying a relationship at all, since I have no idea how it works. The hidden waterworks and I are strangers inhabiting the same body.

A couple years ago, I got a call that my old cat Orson was dying. When I'd moved to Portland from Olympia, he'd stayed with my roommates, but I still felt a parental attachment all these years later. So I made plans to take the train up, to be with him in his final days, to say goodbye.

Before I could buy my ticket, my friend called back to tell me Orson had taken a turn for the worse, that he might die at any moment. She asked if I wanted to talk to him. "On the phone?" I asked. She said sure, why not. So, surrounded by his new owners, people I didn't know, she put me on speakerphone. I'm shy about the phone in general and feel especially uncomfortable being put on speakerphone—even with close friends it feels like I'm suddenly being interviewed for a job, with my every word being monitored. But this was how it had to be. This was goodbye.

"Hey Orson," I said. "I hear you're in pretty bad shape." My voice shook and cracked slightly. "I'm so sorry you're in so much pain." I closed my eyes and imagined him as best I could, imagined him responding to my voice, imagined him feeling the moment in the same way I was feeling it.

"I've been thinking a lot about all the good times we had." I paused as the tears covered my face, the flow of them so unexpected. "And how much joy you brought to so many people." My nose running, I could barely get the words out. "I just want you to know that I love you," I said, as I cried into the silence on the other end.

When I got off the phone, my face still damp, I felt complete in a way I hadn't in years, like I'd had an emotional breakthrough. But then I wondered why this breakthrough had happened with a cat. Why had I cried more for an animal than I had for my lost human loved ones? Perhaps I channeled my grief from other losses into this one because it felt safe—a place where visible grief wasn't demanded, where there was no pressure. The more I thought about it, the breakthrough became questionable, turned strange in my mind.

In the community education writing classes I teach, people cry. I don't push for it to happen or ask students to write about their most vulnerable moments, but every quarter, in each class, at least one person cries. In one class I taught a few years ago, every student cried. Crying happened so regularly they began calling it group therapy.

In the controlled setting of a classroom where I'm the teacher, I've developed an approach to responding to crying. I don't act surprised when it happens, I don't act like it's a fire to be put out, I just let it happen. In my peripheral vision I note other students checking my reaction, and when they see I'm okay with it, they often relax. The tears usually occur when students are reading their work, so when they finish reading or reach a point where they can't go on, I thank them, I nod and make eye contact, letting them know I take it seriously. I give the class a brief moment to feel the weight of what's just been shared, then move on.

I've found that most people don't want a spotlight on them after it happens, they don't want to talk it out, they just want to share what they wrote. They only get embarrassed if we linger too long—making an issue of the crying suggests that it's not a perfectly normal and warranted thing to do. This approach probably doesn't work for everyone, but countless students over the years have told me that they've felt safe crying in my classes. I always thank them and tell them that this is how I hope people will feel, that this is the kind of space I seek to create. But then I go home, wondering about my dry eyes, wondering what it means that I'm able to create that space for others but not for myself.

Some of my favorite crying songs are songs about the desire to not cry. Early soul music is full of these songs. I think of Anna King belting the title refrain of "I Don't Want to Cry," over and over; she can't help but cry, but wishes it was possible, even imaginable, to stop. Etta James's loss was so great that crying was all she could do. John Ellison couldn't stop crying long enough to go outside, too afraid to show his tear-streaked face to the world. At least a dozen male soul singers have wished for rain, so as to hide their tears, the tears they're ashamed of but can't find an end to.

I'm pulled toward these songs with unhinged narrators and their uncontrollable sadnesses. For whatever reason, this kind of grief—so oversized, so constant—resonates with me, and inside I feel that I am this person: destroyed by my emotions, perpetually on the verge of falling apart. Even though, in the self I present to the world, I'm so rarely that person.

Usually I don't worry about the gap between those selves, and I simply hold them as two simultaneous truths. I typically tell people how I'm feeling. I'm open about the emotional trials I'm going through. Being around other people just has a way of putting my more extreme emotions into perspective and calming my worries. If I wasn't the sort of person who worries that my emotional reactions don't manifest publicly like others around me, I probably wouldn't feel like I was lacking.

I read psychology and sociology books about tears. I read about being overcome by tears, tears that won't shut off. I read about performed tears, manipulating others with tears. I read about tears of religious fervor, of anger, of unfathomable loss—a myriad of tears I don't want in my life. I realize what I'm seeking is some universally agreed upon, proper quantity of tears that doesn't exist. I'm wanting to cry about the justified sadnesses at the right moments. To cry more, but not too much.

One night, a family member emails, telling me that my eighty-nine-year-old grandpa—the man I lived with for the first twelve years of my life—has woken up and begun vomiting uncontrollably. He's weak, I learn, with a fever that won't drop, trouble breathing. With no answers as to why, I jump to worst-case scenarios and worry the rest of the night. I go to bed and can't sleep. I imagine all the things I've spent my life trying not to imagine: his decline, what I'll say at his funeral, the great absence he'll leave in my world and what that absence will feel like. Facing the wall, my body shaking, I cry into my pillow. It takes me a second to realize what's happening. I don't try to analyze it. I don't try to stop it or play it up. It's just a quiet moment of release, smaller than any song ever claimed.

[SIXTEEN]

POKED IN THE EYE

A BRIEF HISTORY

SOON AFTER I GOT MY FIRST EYE INJECTION a decade ago, the movie list began. "It reminds me of that scene in *Halloween II*," one person said, emitting a slight shudder. "It makes me think of *The Birds*," said another. Some friends mentioned horror films, titles and directors I'd never heard of, complex and ridiculous scenes of eye harm unlike anything I had watched. Others mentioned obscure art-house films. But most people said "*A Clockwork Orange*, *A Clockwork Orange*," over and over. People told me how it was burned into their minds: the scene with Alex—the stylish young sociopath and leader of a gang of misanthropic dandies—strapped to a chair, eyes clamped open, being overloaded with images of horrific violence.

At least based on the standards of today, the majority of the scenes people mentioned to me weren't especially gruesome, and yet they remembered the scenes with such precision. Their reactions were so strong, so visceral. I'd experienced this with the injections: it wasn't like it was open-heart surgery, it was just a shot, and yet my response was always so oversized, so emotional. Figuring that there must be a connection between my real-life experiences and the similarly intense reactions people have to eye violence on film, I decide to look for clues.

I start before the age of motion pictures, reading the end of Grimm's "Cinderella," where Cinderella's evil stepsisters come to her wedding, trying to ride her good fortune. But as they accompany her and the prince into the church, "the pigeons pecked out one eye from each of them." Then, as they walk out of church after the ceremony, "the pigeons pecked out the other eye from each of them. And thus, for their wickedness and falsehood, they were punished with blindness as long as they lived."

I read pieces of Greek mythology: Oenopion stabbing out Orion's eyes after Orion sexually assaults his daughter. Odysseus getting a cyclops drunk to escape his capture and, when the cyclops falls asleep, stabbing him in the eye with a stake heated in the fire, blinding him. Athena sprinkling cursed water onto Tiresias's face after he sees her bathing. Oedipus, having killed his father and married his mother, gouging his own eyes out.

I read *King Lear* for the scene where Cornwall gouges Gloucester's eyes out, saying, "Lest it see more, prevent it. Out, vile jelly!" Which leads me to look into how theater companies have decided how to portray the eyeballs' vile jelly being removed, everyone worrying over who is watching and how much to show.

I read *Nutcracker* author E. T. A. Hoffmann's 1816 story "The Sandman" about "a wicked man, who comes to children when they won't go to bed, and throws a handful of sand into their eyes, so that they start out bleeding from their heads." Not to be confused with the Mr. Sandman of fifties pop music, Hoffmann's Sandman "puts their eyes in a bag and carries them to the crescent moon to feed his own children, who sit in the nest up there."

In Freud's essay "The Uncanny"—in part working off "The Sandman" story—he claims, "A study of dreams, phantasies and myths has taught us that a morbid anxiety connected with the eyes and with going blind is often enough a substitute for the dread of castration." I laugh when I read this, but I'm also glad to come across a popular theory that recognizes the anxiety we feel around our eyes as being about more than just blindness, in and of itself—hinting at some larger kind of loss of control or identity.

Eventually, I start to watch. I ask a friend to have eye-violence movie nights with me. In his old studio apartment, movie posters covering the walls, mason jars of red wine at our sides, we take in two or three movies at a time. We tell a friend about our new routine, and she coins it "the worst themed–movie night ever." We laugh dismissively, but she's right. Each time I leave his apartment, taking the long walk to the late-night bus line, I feel vaguely awful inside. Not sickened, not castrated, but stripped of something essential.

Between the movie nights and my at-home "research," I watch a dozen films. I watch *May*, a twisted version of an awkward indie rom-com where the film's namesake gouges out her own eye. I watch the dystopian romance *The Lobster*, where a man decides to blind himself to be united with his newly blinded lover. I watch the modern classic of stoner philosophy, *Waking Life*, where a man in a jail cell tells his captors of the eye torture he'll subject them to in hell. I watch *Slumdog Millionaire*, where a boy in India, collected off the street by a corrupt orphanage that makes money by exploiting children, gets his eyes burned out because "blind singers earn double." I watch the film adaptation of Denis Johnson's cult story collection *Jesus' Son*, where a man (played by Johnson himself) walks into a hospital with a hunting knife in his eye—stabbed by his wife for "peeping on the lady next door while she was bathing."

I watch a series of films where the loss of sight turns a person villainous and cruel: the Sandman–inspired *Child Eater* about a man who rapidly loses vision due to macular degeneration and then begins "eating the eyes of kids to keep from going blind"; the below-B cult classic *The Headless Eyes*, where, after losing his own eye, an artist goes on the hunt for other eyes which he then makes into art; and *Anguish*, where an ophthalmologist's assistant suffering from diabetes-related vision loss, under the hypnotic control of his mother, begins murdering people and removing their eyes to somehow delay his blindness.

As I watch these films, it feels like I'm onto something. With each new recommendation, I imagine I'm that much closer to solving it, to understanding. I have no idea what that understanding will be, but I tell myself a revelation is on its way. I just need to put in the hours, absorb the images, figure out how they're operating, what they're saying about our relationships to our bodies. In brief moments of self-aggrandizement, I imagine that what comes out of my studies will be an eye-violence reference point for years to come. But who would reference such a thing, I'm unsure.

*

A friend points me toward Italian horror, which evidently has a fondness for eye violence. I watch a man fire a gun into a peephole and blow a woman's eye and brains out. I watch a zombie gouge a woman's eye out by slowly pulling her head into a long splinter of wood. I watch a different zombie in a different movie by the same director gouge a woman's eye out by slowly pushing the back of her head into a protruding piece of metal.

I google "eye scene," "eye gore," "eye violence," "eye harm." I watch a head get stomped, the eyeball fly out and land in a screaming woman's mouth. I watch a woman, strapped to a doctor's chair, get her eye scorched by a laser. I follow YouTube suggestions. I watch a woman's eye droop wildly from its socket before being gingerly snipped with a pair of sewing scissors. I think about how many of the eyes belong to women, the persistent wet-dream misogyny of male directors, and I wonder what I'm absorbing, how I'll be changed by this.

I read Lina Meruane's autobiographical novel *Seeing Red*. While the narrator awaits an eye surgery to clear up her blood-clouded vision, she flies to Chile to be with her family. On the plane, her partner in a drugged sleep, she runs her fingers over his closed eyelids, separates the lids and touches the "damp, rubbery, exquisite" cornea before she finds herself "licking the whole thing." She says, "I was sucking softly, with my lips, with my teeth, making it mine, delicately, intimately, secretly, but also passionately."

I read Georges Bataille's absurd 1928 counterculture erotica novella *Story of the Eye*, a tale of teenage lovers engaging in "debauchery [that] soils not only my body and my thoughts," but also "the vast starry universe," a book where eyeballs, eggs, and other eye-shaped objects become sex toys.

For a few years in my mid-twenties, eye-touching was a minor kink of mine. I asked lovers if I could touch their eyeballs, or if they could touch mine. It was never an early-in-the-relationship request, but always something that came after a host of other kinks had been explored, and a certain amount of trust had been established. These moments did not happen the moment before orgasm, or even during sex at all. I suppose I was just looking for a new level of intimacy. To me, it was such a vulnerable thing, such an expression of faith in the goodness of the other person. But again and again, my lovers, understandably, reacted in slight horror.

One lover briefly touched my eyeball before immediately recoiling in disgust. Another agreed to let me touch hers, but each time my finger got close, her eye closed. She kept saying, "Okay, this time I've got it." Then, as soon as my finger came near, her eye closed again. Eventually we collapsed in laughter, the sheer ridiculousness of the moment undeniable. "I want to," she said through the laughter, "but my body won't let me."

I begin watching compilations of eye violence—scene after scene, all narrative tension and context removed, eliminating the chance to look away. I sit through all sorts of violations. Thumbs, knives, hypodermic needles, shards of glass, a variety of antiquated tools I'm unfamiliar with. In one film, a cannibal pulls out a living man's eye and eats it. In another, a woman takes her own eye out with a butter knife and a fork. I watch one clip after another, unsure and uninterested in which films they're attached to or who these characters are beyond victims. I don't even like violent movies.

After a few nights of this, I realize I'm watching just to watch, I'm not learning anything. I'm simply putting myself through this strange, self-imposed punishment: viewing the most disturbing scenes from a series of movies for no other reason than to say I did it. My eyes feel like how I imagine Alex's did after his treatments in *A Clockwork Orange*—in some way changed, harmed, done wrong. Or maybe it's my body that feels wronged by my eyes, angry for letting these images in.

In my anger, I wonder if the answer I've been looking for is the one I've had all along: We're protective of our eyes because no sighted person wants to be blind. We flinch more when confronted by harm being done to an eye as opposed to an ear or a nose because we prize vision over all other senses. Eye gouging is also so immediate—so often the end of vision entirely, not just an injury or a partial impairment. Maybe it's as simple as this. But still, I feel there's a revelation I can't seem to get to.

When I turn it all off, I go back to *Seeing Red*, with the narrator having returned to New York to undergo eye surgery. "There were no eye banks, because no one donated dead eyes," Meruane writes. "It was believed . . . that memory lived in them, that eyes were an extension of the brain, the brain peering out through the face to grasp reality. Some people thought the eyes were depositories of memory . . . and others still believed that the soul was hidden there."

I think about these strange, gooey balls, in continual motion, like sugar-fueled children. How alien they seem, but how basic they are to most human connection. I think about what confidence they bring to the sighted, what comfort, what security. And then I think again about their loss.

[SEVENTEEN]

INNERVISIONS

A BRIEF HISTORY

WHEN I WAS YOUNG, MY MOM KEPT ROWS of records on the living room floor, leaning against the back wall of our trailer. They were the first things I saw when I came through the door, the works of art I knew best, statements whose details I memorized, imagining the world both inside and outside of the sleeves' borders. Alongside Joni Mitchell's *Ladies of the Canyon* and Michael Jackson's *Off the Wall* stood Stevie Wonder's *Innervisions,* which was, purely in terms of cover aesthetics, my favorite.

In muted desert browns, a watercolor of Wonder looks out the window of a house with only one wall. His eyelids are closed, face to the sky, a triangular ray projecting from his left eye. Today, knowing more about Wonder's religious beliefs, I interpret the ray in the painting as coming down from the sky and entering Wonder—a gift being bestowed from above. But at the time, as an avid comic book reader, it seemed obvious to me that he had laser vision and was using this laser vision to shoot into outer space. However, unlike in the comics, Wonder's laser did not seem to be a weapon, but rather some kind of peaceful beacon, or healing light. The rocky, barren landscape outside his window implied to me that Wonder might already be on another planet. Perhaps the signal was being sent to Earth, containing a message of everything he'd learned while away.

My family is part of the white audience Motown reached with their crossover soul. My mom and my uncle have listened to Wonder since his Little Stevie beginnings and, to this day, they remain devoted fans. My uncle was the one white guy in a number of funk bands; Wonder was always in the repertoire. He also did Wonder songs in his solo act, and I remember sitting in the park one summer day in the late eighties, at six or seven years old, listening to him sing "Isn't She Lovely," his keyboard and drum machine backing him up, feeling like life couldn't get much better.

Especially at the time, *Innervisions* presented a far different idea of what life for blind people was like than most people imagined. The album offers a portrait of a rich inner world that's aware of what's happening in society, within Black culture, in the mechanisms of racist systematic structures—Wonder doesn't need to see it to experience it. The racial and political tensions of the early seventies informed his lyrics, complicating his usual optimism. On the stark ballad

"Visions" he sings, "Have I lived to see the milk and honey land? Where hate's a dream and love forever stands. Or is this a vision in my mind?" The title of the album, along with the richly imagistic lyrics seemed to imply that, below the surface, there was an internal self, a truer self.

And it's perhaps this—Wonder's tendency to make the public reconsider what they know about the blind—that's fueled the "Stevie Wonder Truthers," a relatively recent internet-driven conspiracy pushing the lie that Stevie Wonder isn't actually blind. According to the most popular theory, what began as a marketing ploy—Motown's infamous founder Berry Gordy trying to cash in on Ray Charles's fame by manufacturing a child virtuoso version, presumably—has turned into an elaborate act that Wonder's had to maintain for the past sixty years.

The Truthers are guided by an assortment of quotidian celebrity observations from the likes of Shaquille O'Neal, Boy George, and Donald Glover, as well as ESPN sports commentator and Truther campaigner Bomani Jones: Wonder likes television, he regularly sits courtside at basketball games, he occasionally directs his eyes toward phone screens, he once took what seemed to be a correctly centered photo of Michael Jackson, he once put his arm around a guy on *The Oprah Winfrey Show* without hesitation, he reportedly wanted to be a contestant on *Dancing with the Stars*, he uses visual imagery in his lyrics. The only halfway interesting bit of evidence is a clip from a 2010 White House performance. In it, Paul McCartney runs across stage, knocks over Wonder's mic stand, and Wonder—though the mic stand isn't touching him or falling directly onto him—reaches out and catches it on its descent with ease.

Watching the videos, reading the news articles, and scrolling through the comments of the Truther blogs is a frustrating reminder of how limited we as sighted people imagine a blind person's life to be. M. Leona Godin writes, "It seems such an obvious thing, once you are blind, to hear smiles and frowns, the direction from which people's voices come from and if they are turned towards you or away, that the surprise sighted people have at such things is at once amusing and alarming."

The common belief that Wonder, or any blind person, can't enjoy TV, can't get more from a basketball game by sitting courtside than in the nosebleeds, can't partner dance, can't feel when someone is close enough to embrace, can't sense a mic stand falling, should widely be seen as offensive. "A blind person has more reason to exploit her human echolocation skills than a sighted person, but that does not mean these skills are superpowers," Godin writes. "[W]hat we often take as superpowers are really just expansions of what humans do unconsciously all the time."

As I've been reading about blindness over the past few years, trying to understand a community I'm not part of but could, at any moment, become part of, I've been regularly staring at the cover of *Innervisions*, thinking about what it said to me as a kid, what it says to me now. What, if anything, it says about blindness. So I look up the cover artist, Efram Wolff, send him an email, and he suggests I give him a call.

From the moment he answers the phone, it's clear to me that the two of us could talk for a long time, that we would likely stray from *Innervisions* many times, and hours could pass if we let them.

Now a sweet, open man in his late sixties, Wolff was a twenty-three-year-old art student in Santa Barbara when he signed a contract to do the artwork for the album. He'd brought his portfolio around to labels on Sunset Boulevard a year or two prior and had done some art for A&M Records, one Motown release—Junior Walker & the All Stars' gorgeous, truly one-of-a-kind *Peace & Understanding Is Hard to Find* cover—and had been slated to do the art for Wonder's previous album, *Talking Book*, but the management had changed their minds at the last minute.

For *Innervisions*, he was only given five days to complete the front cover, gatefold, and back cover, so he worked in a focused frenzy. The only requirement was that they wanted a likeness of Wonder for the cover; the rest was up to him. He did the cover's pencil drawing, drove one hundred miles to LA, and showed it to the art directors. They liked it, so he drove the hundred miles back to Santa Barbara and "proceeded to nonstop work on this" for the next four days, then drove back to LA and turned it in. "I didn't have a lot of time to think about it," he explains.

While the son of German-born Jewish parents who fled at the beginning of the Nazi party's rule is not the person I expected to be behind *Innervisions*' iconically Afrocentric art, Wolff's deep reverence for Black music, his seemingly encyclopedic knowledge of jazz, and his appreciation of African art are immediately obvious. He seems to view the work he did on the album as work he was doing in service of Wonder, rather than something that was distinctly his own.

When I ask him about the ray from Wonder's eyes, he sidesteps the question by telling me it isn't what he would have come up with if he'd had more direction. "They did not tell me that it was going to be called *Innervisions*," he says. "And they were quite secretive about the music; I wasn't allowed to hear anything. It was okay, but it certainly didn't allow me to do anything that related directly to the material. They told me it was going to be called *Visions*. Once I learned it was *Innervisions*, I had a totally different concept of what I would have done for the front cover. But by then it was done."

I ask him if he had the sense that he was working on an album that was in some way commenting on blindness. He tells me he was working with that in mind at times and had modeled the album's inner sleeve on a lithographic print he'd recently done of a blind blues musician being led by a young boy. But many of his considerations were around process—mainly trying to mimic printmaking techniques in watercolors—and letting the art come out of the process. "I can't say there was some really conscious intent," he says. "It was sort of just a visceral working toward creating the piece."

I'm initially disappointed by this—I want an answer, a specific intention, a statement. I've held onto my childhood assumption that the cover was Wonder's concept, not the concept of someone who not only had no contact with Wonder but wasn't even allowed to hear the music his image was representing. But after I get off the phone, I realize it's better this way—the cover's open-endedness, much like the album's concept itself, allowing for so many interpretations, so many possible answers.

Throughout my childhood, Wonder existed as a reference point, mentioned regularly, as if he were a friend of the family, his words invoked as mantras, or vague life lessons.

You know what Stevie says, right? my mom asked before singing, in her rough croon, so similar to my own now, "Everything is alright." *You know what Stevie says?* "Gonna keep on trying, till I reach my highest ground." *You know what Stevie says?* "Here I am, signed, sealed, delivered, I'm yours," she sang, grabbing my hand and spinning me around.

Wonder's music was a staple of our kitchen dance parties. From the outside, my mom and I probably looked more like a *Peanuts* dance party than a *Soul Train* line but, inside, dancing to Wonder was a freedom unlike any other. I still remember moving across the linoleum, "Living for the City" playing, closing my eyes, knowing that the apparent void behind my lids contained more than darkness.

[EIGHTEEN]

ONE OF THE STYLES OF LIVING

A CONVERSATION SERIES

This series uses only the words of the interview subjects, edited down from our longer recorded conversations.

M. SABINE REAR: comic artist, illustrator, zinester, educator

"I keep my art and my living deliberately pretty separate. I like being someone who does five things at once, so for years I was doing retail at two different places, making zines, and doing little art-commission projects. Then I got into the Independent Publishing Resource Center's comics program, and, after I graduated, I took on teaching that program. I also took on an organizing role in the Portland Zine Symposium after tabling there a couple of years. And I like all of these things as their own things. I like making money off my zines, and I like distributing them and getting to benefit from that, but my day job now is disability related.

"I work for the Northwest ADA Center, which is a federally sponsored information center that provides technical assistance around the Americans with Disabilities Act for people in our region. So, anyone can call me and ask a question about the ADA, or often they call me not knowing if their question is about the ADA, but they're just having a disability-related query. I also provide trainings to groups about different aspects of the ADA.

"I was really lucky at the end of college to get to do some disability studies–related events and projects, and those connected me to some disabled artists who are really important to me. I wish I had more blind community, though. I'm good at making community when I know where to go, and with blind community sometimes I've known where to go and sometimes I haven't. I have a couple blind friends that I'm really happy to get to share space with and be creative with, but we don't work on the same types of creative work. I've been lucky to talk to people in one-off conversations about how different experiences of blindness make visual art look and feel different, or mediate what people's way in is, but I am curious about meeting other blind cartoonists or blind illustrators."

"I think the biggest misconception is that I, like many people, call myself blind—I think that identification is important—but I have some sight. And in the spectrum of what's legally considered blindness, I have kind of a lot of sight. So the very 'one thing or the other' idea is that a blind person can't possibly make visual art because all blind people have zero sight. I think even blind people with zero sight can make visual art if they want to—it just may or may not be a potent medium for them. That misconception, and how it leads people down the track of asking kind of the wrong questions, I find a little frustrating.

"For me, and from what I've heard from other blind visual artists, the boundaries of what I can see really inform what I make and what I'm visually interested in. I like to think of my vision as providing stylistic boundaries I can work inside of, and in some ways it's really exciting to not have to choose from everything in the world visually, but to say 'I'm working within the bounds of what I have, and I'm creating a visual language or style that speaks to that.' I think that's interesting, and I want people to find that interesting—rather than just the facts and assumptions of what I can and can't do."

"I want to tell personal stories, often I want to tell stories about blindness; I want to make observations about my experiences, what I think they say about public space, and what I think they say about culture. But I worry about being someone who's presenting a narrative about blindness and embodiment that is separate from living. So I like to come back to fun things I enjoy, like karaoke and professional wrestling. Because when you're making art about yourself you want to remember that you're a whole person—I'm just reminding myself and my reader that, in addition to being a blind lady in the world, I'm also in the world.

"My disability experience informs everything I do to a

certain extent, but it's also informed by all the things I do to bring myself joy. Karaoke, especially. When I think about public space and community-building and having fun, karaoke is such a touchpoint for me. This is where I'm the happiest. It's not the most accessible place in the world—I can only sing karaoke songs I already know all the words to because I can't read the screen—and it's not necessarily in the most accessible buildings all the time. But karaoke is an opportunity to be all-the-way loud, which, as an adult, I don't think you get a chance to do very often.

"Wrestling, similarly, is just big and silly. And I like the opportunity to think deeply about something that's mostly silly. Because those things usually do have some other implications that are worth looking at. But ultimately, at the end of thinking that through, you come back around to 'This is just really fun!' And I like having that in my work. When I'm making work representing myself, I don't want to get too bogged down in creating a version of myself who is only a teachable moment or who is only pointing out experiences of difficulty."

[NINETEEN]

STARING CONTEST

SHE LOOKS AT ME, MOST OFTEN, without smiling. Sometimes she looks interested, other times she looks unimpressed. Usually she just stares. Babies typically don't start smiling—as in, not just smiling as a reflex, but out of joy—until at least six weeks, sometimes a few months. And now, at four-and-a-half months, it's true: she does occasionally smile. But these smiles still don't come all that often.

Her mom calls her *the critic*. She's not a difficult baby but she's also not, like many, easily amused. She takes the world in without much reaction—a quality I can appreciate. I respect her more because she's not easy to please, because she seems to be trying to absorb rather than change her surroundings. She's the child of a writer, and to me it shows. This is what writers do: Watch the world closely. Take things in. See it all, let it pass through the body, and try to make meaning from it.

*

Lately, I've been staring a lot. I do some of it at night, staying up deep into the witching hours with the person I'm falling in love with, but I do even more during the days, poorly rested but alert, looking into the oversized eyes of the baby. The baby isn't mine. She's the new daughter of a close friend who's paying me to be there while she tries to sleep, to feed herself, to pump milk from her body, to do the most basic tasks of life she has suddenly found herself unable to do while caring for her kid.

The month before giving birth, she realized she was going to be raising her baby alone and asked me to nanny for her. Though my pieced-together manner of making ends meet is well known among my friends, nannying isn't a service I typically offer. But my friend knew I'd spent my adolescence babysitting my brother and sister who were born when I was a teenager, she knew I was struggling financially, and she trusted me. So I said yes. How could I not? To get paid, by someone I adore, to be with her baby—I couldn't imagine anything better, anything I wanted in my life more.

To most people, it's probably an odd choice: a part-time community college instructor in his mid-thirties doing a job most often associated with teen girls. I don't have kids and don't plan to. I'm broke (still). People most often assume I'm either hanging out with the baby as a free service to a struggling friend or that I'm in a relationship with her mom—neither of which are true. Even after a full summer of nannying, people still don't seem to understand it. Just the other day, after a few drinks, my party-aunt asked me, loudly, in a room full of other family members, "So, when are you going to marry this single mom?"

But these sorts of outside misreadings and misunderstandings fall away as soon as I arrive in the morning. I've become curious about every bit of the baby-caring process, and, when the baby sleeps on my lap, I google with my free hand all the questions that have been building up in my brain. Every phone app I use now tries to sell me baby stuff, every YouTube commercial seems to start with the word *fatherhood* (always spoken with the same measured tone of male confidence, regardless of the product), and my friends and family keep expressing their slight bafflement as I fall deeper in, enjoying it more, working as much as I can.

In recent months, I've started to say *I love staring*, which no one quite knows what to make of. I know it sounds strange. Wrong, even. Especially given that I'm a white man in a culture that gives white men a lot of power to stare, or at least the ability to stare and not face many consequences.

Most people typically think of staring as something unasked for, something that one person does selfishly, unconcerned that it's making another person feel uncomfortable. But I don't like making anyone feel uncomfortable, and a very large percentage of my life has been spent figuring out ways to avoid bringing discomfort to the people around me. So my recent embrace of staring—one of the most dependable ways to make another person feel awkward or in danger—has concerned and surprised even me.

I've come to believe that there are two distinct, though perhaps obvious, categories of staring: *staring at* and *staring with. Staring at* is what we do when we give in to our curiosity, shock, or desire, choosing not to worry about how it makes the one being stared at feel. I don't believe this is always an awful, offensive thing—our eyes are naturally drawn to novel sights, things we haven't seen before—but at its core, *staring at* is a selfish action, personally satisfying at the potential cost of someone else's comfort.

Staring with is mutually agreed upon. It's not to be confused with eye contact—something you do to acknowledge someone, or to gauge or affirm interest. To truly stare with someone, a mutual agreement must be reached. If you try to stare with and the other person isn't into it, you're suddenly just staring at.

I meet some friends for drinks and they ask me how the job is going. *Mostly we just stare*, I tell them. They look at me uncertainly. *I love staring*, I say.

Pre-fight "staredowns" are a fixture of mixed martial arts matches. Initially created as a gimmick to get viewers to tune in early, staredowns have become nearly as popular as the fights themselves. Their basic premise—a childhood staring contest being played by oversized adults—makes them addicting. With faces inches apart, opponents look into each other's eyes. Some raise fists, some trash-talk, some dance around, while others just stare. It's the simplest form of intimidation, "visual violence," an act seemingly primal.

For most of my life, staring has made me uncomfortable. There were so many other kids, particularly boys, searching out the wallflower. The shy kid was an easy target—a fun game to play when they needed a boost of confidence. And most often, the entry point to the game was the eyes. Stare at the shy kid until he can't help but look. And then: *What are you looking at? What's your problem?* After my first few years of public school, I figured out ways to deflect. I didn't get flustered like so many of the other kids when prodded, didn't make myself interesting to pick on. But mean kids still tried, I still felt their eyes, still feared accidentally engaging with their stares.

"Our heart rate increases when we are stared at; being subjected to a stare even registers on a cortical EEG [electroencephalograph]," Rosemarie Garland-Thomson writes in her book *Staring: How We Look*. "So viscerally potent is the staring encounter that we can even feel stares directed at us. In fact, humans from infancy can detect unseen stares. We not only believe that we can tell when we are being stared at, but repeated experiments dating as early as the nineteenth century suggest that, in fact, we do. Staring, then, has vivid physiological effects for both starer and staree that emanate from the neural automata and spread through the entire body."

I've always felt the power of the stare, and I failed at holding even a friendly gaze for most of my childhood. But once, at a slumber party in fifth grade, after several rounds of telephone and truth-or-dare, a staring contest started up. When my turn came, I figured I would promptly lose and return to my role as shy spectator. But as I looked into my friend's eyes and felt the rush of vulnerability that typically made me look away, I realized this was not just a challenge but also an opportunity. It was a chance to look freely without worrying about being judged for simply wanting to look. One after another, I outstared each of my friends at the party. And with each friend, each pair of eyes, the act revealed an inner secret they carried—a secret I didn't have words for, but could sense.

It wasn't a feeling I experienced again until I was fifteen and at the beginning of my first real relationship. One of the great joys of falling in love for the first time was being able to stare openly. Barely out of my shell, it felt like such a risk to open up like that. Being sexual, sharing my hidden inner world, looking deep into my love's eyes. On her bed, upstairs in her mom's drafty old farmhouse, we lay on our sides, face to face, the muted afternoon light of rural Washington coming through the windows, slowly darkening as time passed and our mutual infatuation grew. It was some sort of freedom—vulnerability, the dream I'd been dreaming of, offering itself to me.

Stare enough and you begin to realize how much of the emotional part of staring is simply seeing yourself reflected in the other person's eyes. During her three-month retrospective at the Museum of Modern Art, performance artist Marina Abramović sat and stared with over fifteen hundred people. "I am just a trigger," she said afterward, "I am just a mirror and actually they become aware of their own life, of their own vulnerability, of their own pain, of everything.

"It was much better if the people sat longer than shorter because there was more time to work with the material, with the energy. When they sit for a short time, it's kind of a short investment and they can't get as much out of it. For me, it's very important that I create the kind of circumstances in the space that when people come into that zone they actually forget about the time. And this really happened—people came and sat with me for forty minutes and they were thinking it was ten minutes, so they lost the sense [of time]."

I started the job four months ago, when the baby was twenty days old. At first, she couldn't focus her eyes. I had no idea what she was seeing, but as I held that tiny human in my lap, we locked eyes. I explained to her what little I knew of the broader world and told her about her smaller world, her exhausted and brilliant mom, the tiny house they lived in, the things she might experience in the years to come. I read to her from Gertrude Stein's bizarre children's book and a Bette Davis biography. I occasionally considered existential dilemmas aloud, our responsibility to other humans, the opportunities we have to show care in small ways, but mostly we just looked at each other.

In life, I tend to rush through the world. My mind has a tendency to drift into the thing I have to do next, the ways I'm falling behind, and I'm often in my head, distracted. When I tell people I'm nannying an infant, friends—especially friends with children—love to tell me it's a boring age. That babies in the first several months are humans without personality. But the baby had an obvious personality the first time I met her, before she was even three weeks old. And I've been anything but bored. Sometimes I attempt to make our staring into a contest—a game we're playing for fun, or out of a desire to win—more than some wholesome way of connecting or figuring each other out. But that game never lasts for long; I always give in to the pressure. She always wins.

*

Finally, there comes a bleary-eyed workday when I stop trying to wax poetic to a tiny person who can't stop me, and I just decide to quietly be. I lie on the floor, put some Raffi on, and the baby and I use our eyes. Occasionally I give her a small toy or object and she focuses in on that, as if there are worlds inside it, an entire history in the rattle's curves, or the pacifier's give and squish. Then she looks at me, and immediately forgets about the thing in her hands. We stare, and I'm struck, my heart full. *This is something*, I think. *This gift.*

[TWENTY]

A MACHINE FOR WRITING

A BRIEF HISTORY

THE STORY OF THE TYPEWRITER BEGINS in the early nineteenth century with Pellegrino Turri inventing a machine for his friend, a young countess who had recently gone blind, so she could write letters. Or it begins in the mid-nineteenth century when a Danish pastor comes up with a writing ball that resembles a giant metal pincushion. Or perhaps it begins a century before either of those, in England, with an engineer patenting "an artificial machine" for "transcribing letters singly or progressively one after another, as in writing"—a machine he may have built, but likely just imagined.

In the 150 years before the typewriter reached mass production and public consciousness, there were a wealth of different origin stories and nearly a hundred inventors: a medical doctor in New York, the head of an institution for blind people in England, a bicycle inventor in Germany, a priest in Brazil. Its many origin stories are representative of its history as a whole: unclear, messy, up for debate.

Many if not most of the early inventors were working on a tool for people who were blind. Some of them sought to develop a machine on which the blind could create clear text to correspond with the sighted—without concerns about uniformity of script or whether the quill had the proper amount of ink—while others conceived of a machine that would emboss paper so blind people could read their own writing. Several inventors tried to combine these concepts by making each key activate two arms or plungers, striking or perforating separate sheets of paper, but all these attempts were too complex to be wholly successful.

Many early machines had keyboards laid out alphabetically, some mimicked the piano or harpsichord's design, one wrote in syllables instead of letters. They were often large, awkward, and very slow. An early French writing machine was advertised as "almost as fast as a pen," and *Scientific American* called an early American prototype "perfectly efficient except as to the element of time."

I began collecting typewriters by accident. It started in the early 2000s, when I co-ran a small nonprofit poetry press in Olympia with my childhood friend Cole. Both of us resistant to the oncoming push toward digital, we became dedicated to physical objects and print media and insisted that the interiors of all our publications be typed on a typewriter. Maybe we did this because we were young enough to have never used typewriters for schoolwork but old enough that they had been around our houses—machines we viewed as toys. Or because of our all-too-common reverence for the Beats. Or because of that photo of Bob Dylan typing away at a little table, his legs crossed. Or the one of Anaïs Nin at her typewriter, staring off, daydreaming. The reasons for our attachment to these machines were of little importance to us—our adoration didn't need an origin story.

Your average history of the typewriter typically begins in the Midwestern United States with Christopher Latham Sholes, who, it's often claimed, solved the issue of speed. Sholes's 1868 patent of the "type-writer"—the name that finally stuck after a baffling array of individual writing-machine monikers—was deemed the first machine practical for wide-scale production, largely because of the QWERTY keyboard system Sholes devised. The seemingly random configuration of letters on Sholes's keyboard was a purely mechanical solution, implemented to avoid frequently used letters interfering with each other and causing jams.

Five years later, E. Remington & Sons manufactured Sholes's patent, and that's where many histories end. The implication here is that Remington took this minor risk, surely knowing all along it would work out, and the world greeted the typewriter with open arms.

But early designs were still slower than writing by hand. Remington went through nearly forty versions in the first six years. All were riddled with defects: carriages jumped, typebars jammed, weights broke and fell. Remington nearly abandoned them as a commercial failure. "Resistance to the machine was ubiquitous," writes the great typewriter historian Michael H. Adler, "and the task of the inventor was a thankless one." What now seems like a relatively simple device was one of the most complex consumer machines of the time, containing over two thousand parts. Most people couldn't wrap their minds around the machine or why they would want to use one, let alone own one.

One time, when Cole was staying in our rural hometown without a typewriter, I brought one up on the bus and carried it along a bike trail for miles just so we could put out an issue of our free monthly poetry zine. It was only when I arrived at the trashed flophouse where he was staying, behind a pallet factory deep in the country, my arms rubbery and body covered in sweat, that I realized our romanticism might be foolish.

The typewriter we most often used for the press wasn't a beautiful old manual, but rather a faded electric. It was by no means handsome, and its motor whined like a weed eater, but it was reliable. There was poetry here, and together we saw it: childhood friends, now adults with a nonprofit press—paperwork and everything—living miles below the poverty line but getting words out into the world. I remember opening the typewriter's case on a milk crate flipped on its side—our trash-house worktable for the weekend—unveiling our baby-blue beast. How Cole and I smiled at each other, our faces radiant. The machine was a symbol of our commitment: to poetry, to the past, to each other. There was nothing foolish about it.

*

Initially, Remington marketed the typewriter as something housewives could use around the home—essentially a busy-work appliance or a plaything—and under this campaign the machine sold horribly. It was only when typewriter trainings for women started spreading across the country that the machine's fate began to change. Suddenly, there were people who knew how to use the machines, leading not only to them becoming more common in offices, but giving women an opportunity to enter the workforce on a grand scale.

This societal change was predictably met with fierce opposition, exploitation, and limited mobility. While typewriter companies and popular media were selling a glamorous image of the "type-writer girl," creating a steady flow of new employees, corporations were restructuring themselves to ensure that the new typists would make far less than their male counterparts and never advance to management. And yet, the typewriter was also said to have enabled women to transcend many of the gender-based barriers commonly associated with the act of writing, which led to more opportunities for female novelists, poets, and playwrights. The machine was a very complex, very mixed blessing.

The blessing was perhaps just as mixed for blind people, those who were initially positioned to benefit the most from this new technology. Although the typewriter gave them the power to create clear text to correspond with the sighted, it also led to a more visually based society where the written word occupied an even more dominant position. And while a fully functional braille typewriter was created in the 1890s, it wasn't until the 1950s that one reached mass production.

Early histories of the typewriter didn't see anything complex in its blessing. One screed from 1918 repeatedly asserted that the typewriter had not only freed "the busy executive from the bondage of the pen," but also "freed the world from pen slavery." An article from the same year in the magazine *Typewriter Topics* claimed that "the typewriter undoubtedly has been more instrumental in the world's progress than anything else." Remington immediately worked both these assertions into their advertising and added that their product also completed "the economic emancipation of womankind."

Today, when it's not being dismissed as having been a necessary but prosaic step toward the computer, the typewriter is celebrated as an icon of artistic creation and poetic freedom. It's an artful symbol that graphic designers embrace when they want to imply a certain whimsy, or the feeling that the guy with the old-timey hat typing poems on the sidewalk in the touristy part of town provides and cashes in on. However, for the first century of its existence, the typewriter was associated almost solely with the business world. It didn't show the personality of the user in the way that handwriting does—it was cold, hard, made of steel, and used for office-work drudgery. It was the antithesis of the monetarily unconcerned free expression we associate with poetry and creative thought. Many authors refused to use the machines, even a generation or two after their popularity was firmly established. Their reluctance to embrace the technology was essentially the same as that of those contemporary writers and artists who champion the typewriter as an inspiring alternative to the inhuman computer.

As the years went by, I accumulated more and more typewriters. I found a Remington Rand from the forties buried in a pile of small household appliances at Value Village. I bought a sixties Olympia De Luxe at a yard sale. I spotted an Underwood No. 5 from the thirties on some friends' back porch, rusting in a rain-soaked cardboard box, and they told me to take it home. Most of the typewriters in my collection were gifts—friends leaving me theirs when they moved away or placing them in my care for semipermanent safekeeping as they went on adventures. I don't know how to fix them, I can barely change the ribbon, I only have a loose knowledge of the common brands, and I'm painfully slow at typing, but somehow I became the typewriter guy.

Calling my ramshackle pile a collection is, at best, questionable. At its peak, I maybe had a dozen, and in the last year or two I've been giving them to friends on the same sort of permanent-loan basis under which I acquired most of them. In my tiny basement room, with so few other possessions, the number of typewriters lining the shelves had begun to hint at an unhealthy obsession.

Adler lauds Pellegrino Turri as the machine's true inventor. In the early 1800s, the Italian gifted a typewriter to his friend Countess Carolina Fantoni da Fivizzano so she could write letters. After the Countess's death, her writing machine was passed on to the late inventor's son and its history ends there, its fate unknown. But Turri's son donated some of the Countess's typewritten letters to a local historical archive, and those sixteen preserved letters demonstrate the impressive efficiency of his father's invention, which perhaps worked better than most of the other writing machines that came after it, machines that, as Adler puts it, "worked badly, in varying degrees of badness."

Depending on the source, the relationship between Turri and the Countess is described as being either the story of two dear friends, or an affair between two star-crossed lovers, separated by distance, each married to the wrong person. Unsurprisingly, the latter version tends to attract more excitement than the former. Given the contents of the sixteen preserved letters—chaste on the surface with potentially suggestive undertones—both scenarios are equally likely, and since, as Adler points out, early typewriter history was "a kind of happy historical anarchy in which general ignorance was interpreted as license for perverting the facts to suit any purpose," I believe there's room for their story to become whatever we'd like it to be. Carey Wallace's charming 2010 novel *The Blind Contessa's New Machine* imagines Turri and the Countess negotiating a complex, tortured love affair, and this particular interpretation of their relationship seems to have ossified in the internet age: *The typewriter began as a symbol of love, an elaborate gift to a blind woman from the sighted man who loved her.*

Maybe that's the true origin, or maybe it's a myth. Or maybe the desire for it is just the result of a limitation we've put on our stories: that romantic love trumps all, that dedicated friendship doesn't carry the narrative weight to land with the necessary force. But I want to believe that love stories can be about more than just romance, that we could say: *The typewriter began as a symbol of friendship, an invention to make a friend's transition into blindness a little less difficult*, and it would be enough. I want to believe that a person created a machine not to achieve notoriety, fame, and fortune—like so many writing-machine inventors who came after him—but to simply help a friend in need.

[TWENTY-ONE]

KINGDOM OF THE SICK

IN LATE 2018, I FLY TO PHILADELPHIA ALONE. To save money on the ticket, I travel overnight, crossing the country, with multiple layovers, sleeping on the floors of airports. Fourteen hours later I walk into a university lobby—red eyes, messy hair, wrinkled work clothes—on time to the minute. Signing in, I try not to feel self-conscious about being here on a scholarship. One result of growing up low-income is that I'm not good at being given things. I worry I'll disappoint, that I won't live up to the expectations a gift implies. I worry someone will see me—a boyish mess of a man—and say, "*You're* the one we gave money to?" And I'll have to say, "Yes, yes, I don't know why I'm here either."

The conference is for members of PXE International, the advocacy group I joined ten years ago in my early frenzy for knowledge about my condition. I'm a member of PXE International in the barest sense of the word. I've referenced their website a few times over the years, used it to fact-check myself when writing about PXE, emailed them a few questions a few years ago. I don't take their surveys, rarely read their newsletters—I don't participate in the community at all.

But, by chance, I opened the newsletter that announced the conference's registration at exactly the right moment. I was trying to finish the book I was writing about eyes, vision, and blindness—a book, in part, about PXE—and I wanted, more than anything, to be around others with similar concerns, similar struggles. Despite several attempts, I'd never met anyone else with the condition, and I especially wanted to meet older people to get some small peek into what the future might hold. When I saw that the registration fee was out of my slim budget, my glee dropped, but I worked up the courage to ask if they had scholarship options, expecting to be rejected. They wrote back, telling me of a generous donor who had just given money for this very purpose. They couldn't cover my plane ticket or a room, but I could attend for free. Though I was still unsure how to pay for the parts of the trip they couldn't cover, I accepted their offer.

Waiting in the lobby while others arrive, I scan the room, knowing most of the people here are my people, the people I've been wanting in my life. It's overwhelming. I'm too tired to put on my extrovert mask, so I play wallflower, reading a local alt-weekly while leaning against a pillar. A put-together woman with short white hair approaches and asks if I'd like to join their conversation, and suddenly I'm with a group of welcoming middle-aged women, comparing stories, my first time so easy, subdued, quiet. If I was a different kind of person, I would celebrate—hug, give kisses on the cheek, shout out my complex affection for this identity we share. But I'm not that person, and they've all met before, all previously been to this conference. To them, I'm just another person with PXE.

Still, they ask. So I tell them about my eyes, the treatments, and they know all about it, though few of them have experienced hemorrhages. My realization that we're living with similar-but-different conditions begins with the discussion of pain. They question me about joints, about leg cramps, about constricting vessels, about heart irregularities, and I say no, I didn't even know any of that was possible. They ask me how old I am and when I tell them thirty-six, one says, "You would have had them by now."

Someone else says, "Oh, they just haven't hit yet."

After everyone has arrived, our big group walks to a restaurant a few blocks away. We move slowly. There are fewer white canes than I'd expected, but more walking canes. When I tell my new friends that I call PXE "my eye condition" as shorthand, they frown. It's not really that, they say, explaining that simplifying the disease so severely doesn't provide a true picture of its scope. I nod, understanding my misunderstanding.

Though I've been aware that the disease causes calcification in the eyes, skin, intestines, and blood vessels, nearly all the PXE-related studies I've read have been about the issues it causes in the retina. And so, I've been dismissive of these other potential consequences; skin was just cosmetic, gastrointestinal issues were uncommon, and I'd imagined the circulatory system was a concern for just a small number of patients, something rarer still. But now, sitting in a private room at an Italian restaurant, one person after another is telling me that their biggest issue is not the eyes, but rather the legs, the vessels running through the body. The pain, which I don't have. Yet.

*

Though I may have failed to find other people with PXE in real life before now, when I joined the PXE International Facebook group a week before the conference, I learned that they were digitally there all along. As I scratched the surface, I found out that people with PXE, adorably, refer to themselves as "pixies," that the range of topics they discussed was vast, and that more people than I expected were preoccupied with the cosmetic side of the disease. But I stopped there. *You'll learn more soon*, I told myself.

The truth is, PXE, at the moment, isn't my primary concern. The preventative injections, which I'm tentatively trying out more and more, have been doing their job, and—though I still don't get the treatments as often as my doctor wants me to—I haven't had a hemorrhage in over a year. I've had a scare or two, but no actual bleeds. My sight is largely intact. But while my PXE has become, at least momentarily, a background worry, a new issue has taken its place.

It began in the early spring when I went to a show and almost fainted. I was up front, sober, well-hydrated, nodding my head along to the songs. A post-punk band that had been broken up for nearly thirty years was playing a reunion show, and despite being loud and sold out, the audience was too old for it to be wild. There was no dancing, no mosh pit, I wasn't being squished. But then, out of nowhere, I began to wobble. My head nods turned into a grandfather clock's metronomic swing. I grabbed the shoulder of the stranger next to me, a towering metalhead, before my vision went. The club bleached white, fuzzy, a broken TV's hiss, the room narrowing quickly. Following this thin tunnel, I broke through the crowd, an apparent drunk stumbling toward some sudden purpose that no one else could see or understand. I landed in a folding chair against the wall of the club, covered in sweat, as the room gradually opened, coming back into focus. The eyes of everyone standing along the wall looked down at me, wide. Though I didn't know it at the time, this was the beginning of a sickness.

I made an appointment that turned into a series of tests that turned into another appointment, another series of tests. I was still making it to work and class, but I was more exhausted than I had ever been in my life. Before this, I'd never been able to take naps, but suddenly I was getting home after a couple hours of writing at the coffee shop and collapsing onto the couch like I'd spent the morning training for a triathlon, often not getting up for hours. I was falling asleep on the bus, I was weak, barely able to eat, I tried mowing the lawn a few times—a tiny square in a residential neighborhood—and each time gave up after a couple passes.

At first the doctors thought it was an infection, then a parasite, then—when the exhaustion faded and the indigestion sharpened—irritable bowel syndrome, IBS. The previous November, a weight in my stomach had appeared. A rock, sitting firmly in the middle of my gut, all day and night, immovable. After a number of tests, I was diagnosed with IBS—a condition there's no test for and which is determined by process of elimination. I didn't believe the diagnosis at the time, nor did I believe what I was currently going through was IBS-related. I'd read about IBS and this was bigger: I knew it, even if the doctors didn't.

After months of tests, my insurance finally approved a referral to a specialist. I'd been unable to eat solid foods for most of the previous month, had lost twenty pounds off my already small frame, I looked noticeably unwell. The specialist told me that, given all the tests I'd gone through, we had eliminated nearly all the possible explanations. It was either Crohn's disease or cancer. A couple weeks later, I celebrated when I was diagnosed with Crohn's.

The morning after the welcome dinner, seventy or eighty of us gather in a high-ceilinged room with big windows and good natural light to listen to the small number of researchers working directly on PXE. I take note of specific genes and genetic terms. "Missense, nonsense, indel, splicing," I write, unsure of what the words mean. I jot down quotes that seem significant: "know your mutation," "redundant and sagging skin," "bad neck."

Everyone has a diagnosis story and most often that story starts with the neck. Calcium deposits form bumps in the neck, and for many, this is the first hint of the problem hidden within. I look around and study all the bumpy necks, a whole room of us. *Cobblestone*, they call it, an *unwashed look*. A conference of permanently dirty-looking necks. But I notice that each person's markings are different. My neck is a more or less uniform series of small bumps, but there's a woman with patches of large bumps alongside wide smooth stretches. There's a woman who used to call it a birthmark. A woman who thought it was the result of a burn she'd suffered as a child. Sitting there, I begin to understand that the online group's focus on cosmetic concerns is largely gendered. Before now, I'd never considered what it would be like to be a woman with PXE—as the vast majority of those diagnosed are—what it would be like to have a cobblestone neck and to try to fit within conventional female beauty standards, to have the bumpy parts of my body scrutinized in the way women's bodies are. As I scan the room, a doctor explains that many patients consider or try plastic surgery, but that the PXE eventually whittles away at the smoothed-over section of skin, turning it "redundant and sagging" once again, and I vow to no longer dismiss the disease's cosmetic side.

After lunch, we crowd into small classrooms for breakout sessions with the researchers. We ask *Is this PXE-related?* about a huge range of health issues. *Trouble breathing? Weak teeth? Difficulty differentiating colors? Sensitivity to overhead lights? Toe pain? Thigh cramping? Debilitating fatigue?*

When a woman describes her fatigue, I'm reminded of the previous evening, when multiple people told me how they've always been unable to keep up physically. In school, they wore out before the other kids, were always mediocre at sports. All day long, the word *fragile* has been coming up. How we're more fragile than other people. All our fragile retinas. The fragile, narrow vessels running through our bodies. Our fragile, bumpy skin. Our fragile guts.

I take everybody's concerns seriously, especially since I have a pile of my own, but at some point I can't help but wonder if maybe we're all hypochondriacs. Has the diagnosis of our shared rare disease made us more conscious of every ache, every situation when our bodies don't act ideally? We'll probably never know where the limits of the disease begin and end—what's being a PXE patient and what's being a human in a body.

*

I've been on steroids for Crohn's-related gastrointestinal inflammation for a while now. What was initially supposed to be five weeks has stretched into five months, and each time I try to wean myself off them, the pain comes back. I imagine the inflammation as a small, sleeping animal—a weasel, typically—and I'm tiptoeing around it, trying not to wake it. According to the doctors, the fact that I can't get off the steroids is a sign that I need to switch to a more permanent solution: bimonthly, three-hour infusions of drugs made from the DNA of humans and mice. Initially, I can't imagine having to rely on yet another relatively new oddity of medical science, but several weeks later I find myself in a waiting room, getting vaccinations to prepare for a lifetime of infusions.

When an elderly woman with white hair and a walker comes to the check-in window, the receptionist tells her she has her appointment times mixed up. "But it makes sense why you would be confused," the receptionist says, "you have an appointment every day this week." The white-haired woman shakes her head. Punctuating each word with disbelief, she repeats, "Every. Day. This. Week."

Her life isn't mine, but I feel a kinship. Between ophthalmologist appointments, eye injections, general practitioner appointments, gastrointestinal specialist appointments, phone appointments, calls to schedule appointments, lab tests, colonoscopies, endoscopies, MRIS, CAT scans, OCT scans, pharmacy pickups, and emails with my doctor, I've interacted with the medical system nearly every day for the past six months. If there was an end in sight, it might not seem like such a big deal; I might be able to laugh it off.

I've never smoked cigarettes, never been a big drinker. I spent the first few years of my early twenties as a pretty dedicated stoner, but I haven't smoked much pot or done many other drugs for years. I generally don't even take over-the-counter medications. I've eaten a mostly plant-based diet since my early teens, taken herbs and vitamin supplements. I walk several miles each day, work in the yard on a regular basis, work out. I'm not obsessive about health, have never been strict or uptight, am not one to preach. What I'm trying to say is that I'm not the person you would expect to be sick and not the person whose sickness feels like poetic justice for self-righteous behavior. My body is simply attacking itself in a variety of ways. Based on what we know of Crohn's and autoimmune disorders, it wouldn't matter whether I spent the past thirty-six years as a health nut or a junk-food addict. I would still have Crohn's. And I would still have PXE.

At the conference, one of the researchers uses the term "bad genes" and, though it initially seems slightly rude—a judgment on our families, or at least our ancestors—I come to hold onto the term, to identify with it. "Bad genes" covers it all: my bad eyes, my bad digestion, my bad skin, my bad circulation.

Lately, Susan Sontag's well-worn line from *Illness as Metaphor* has been bouncing around in my mind, like the chorus of a song, stuck in my head. "Everyone who is born holds dual citizenship," she writes, "in the kingdom of the well and the kingdom of the sick." And at the conference, or in the waiting room, or facing yet another needle, another test, I feel more a part of the kingdom of the sick than the well.

I've spent nearly a year unwell. And it's okay, I'm living, I'm fine. I get up in the morning and I get my errands done, I go to work. But I have to skip my friends' readings and shows, I skip seeing my favorite bands and authors, I skip the birthday parties, I skip most social interactions that require me to hang out with more than one person, or any situation where it would be difficult to tell people, "I'm sick. This is hard." This isn't the true kingdom of the sick, I know. This isn't the cancer or TB death sentence Sontag wrote about. But it's at least somewhere in between the sick and the well, a place without a clear definition or community, a place that's less severe, but still lonely.

Attendance is sparse on the final day of the conference. Many have already departed Philadelphia, due back in their respective cities to get ready for work tomorrow morning, but the rest of us gather, trying to carry on the energy of the weekend in a room that has more chairs empty than filled. The head of the organization leads the day. She's charming and passionate, a minor celebrity in this community, with a viral TED Talk about PXE and collaboration in the sciences that's perhaps the only popular reference point for the disease. We ask about the potential treatments, the experimental preventative measures, all the ways we could be trying harder. "But the question is," she asks in return, "do you want to have medical lives?" She goes on to differentiate between *living* versus *living in perpetual worry*, and my head fills.

I think about all the years I pretended I didn't have the disease, the years I ignored the few recommendations I knew of. I think of all the eye supplements I haven't taken, the decade of online PXE group posts I've missed. I think of the countless online groups for Crohn's I haven't even glanced at, all the guessing I've done since being diagnosed with both diseases. The daily experiments of eating and drinking, exercising, trying. There's so much to know, so many variables I could be accounting for—where's the line between being informed and being negligent?

A woman stands up and says, "We're more brittle than other people." I missed the context, don't know if I agree, or want to agree, but when she looks me in the eyes, I nod in return.

I fly home from the conference, get off the plane, get on a bus, and arrive just in time to stand in front of a classroom. This quarter, in one of my community education writing classes, I have a student who is blind. A soft voice, a mustache and a ponytail, his own quirky sense of humor, we navigate all the small ways I design my classes with the expectation that my students will be able to see. Notes on the board, handouts, workshop papers, my tendency to rely on nonverbal gestures and facial expressions. I stay on top of it, but it's challenging, and even a little fun. It's also a wake-up call—all this meditating on blindness and yet so little practical experience. Some nights, as I fumble through unexpected challenges in class, it feels like blindness is just an idea to me, a theme to explore on the page, to consider metaphorically.

One night, my student stays after class. While I move the chairs and tables back to their usual places, he asks me about the "book about eyeballs," a cheeky phrase I'd used in some online bio that now sounded clumsy to my ears, even insensitive. I tell him about the years I've spent thinking about eyes and sight, the disease that might make me blind, and he smiles politely. It occurs to me that for a person who's already blind, there might not be much drama in the mere possibility of losing one's sight. "You know what the worst part of being blind is?" he asks. "Everyone thinks it's a miracle that you can do anything at all. Even the simplest thing, someone will say, 'Wow, you're doing so well.' Most people seem to assume I'm not only blind, but also dumb."

I think of all the times I've likely done some version of this. Not only with him, but with my blind cousin, with all the blind people I've met throughout my life, all the blind people with whom I've shared bus trips and waiting rooms. *You're doing great*, I've said as I held the door for them, as if they were small children in need of encouragement. I want to ask him if it's lonely, but it seems like an intrusive question, something too big for me to unpack, so I let the moment pass. Instead, I shout "You're a miracle!" as he walks out the door, and he laughs.

The week after the quarter ends, the federal government threatens to drop me and millions of other people from our health insurance plans. Suddenly I'm back to wondering: How will I pay for the eye injections if I get dropped? What about the infusions? If I stop paying for the infusions first, will my Crohn's flare up again? Will I have to go back to a liquid diet? I think about the existential fragility of having to rely on medical science, of being permanently dependent on a drug called "vascular endothelial growth factor" and another called "anti-tumor necrosis factor." *What will I do when the apocalypse comes?* I wonder, imagining having to navigate without sight, unable to eat without pain, all the worst-case scenarios. But I snap myself out of it, telling myself I'm a catastrophizer in an able body, uncomfortable—

like all humans—with uncertainty. I'm aware that this is, quite simply, life: attempting to make order out of chaos, trying to avoid getting mentally stuck in what might be.

So much of my fear of being sick is based on the fear of being alone. I've been single for years now, and the years have made me more introverted, more set in my ways. Being sick has killed my sex drive and, largely, my desire to be partnered. It's hard not to worry about what life might look like if the worst-case arrives and I'm by myself. I have enough friends and family that this isn't fully rational, but the fear of loneliness is powerful, capable of suppressing all reason.

When I was a kid, I was preoccupied with happiness. It bothered me that any moment could become flawed. An eyelash could fall into your eye, you could spill your soda, a dream could end just when it was getting good. I couldn't take it. Happiness was fleeting, it never stuck around. And in my year of being sick, I've realized that, even for the healthiest person, health is also fleeting. We're all more fragile than we imagine we are—each day is just a series of physical and emotional highs and lows where we search out some semblance of balance that sticks around for a few brief moments before leaving without warning.

At the infusion center—a hidden friendly clubhouse in the middle of an ugly impersonal hospital—my favorite nurse secures the IV with bright red medical tape. "To match your pants," she says, and I smile, then head to the kitchen with my IV pole to grab graham crackers, peanut butter, and two juice boxes, preparing myself to sit for two or three hours. On the way back to my room, I pass by my neighbors, cancer patients living with a deep uncertainty I can't imagine. Later, I go downstairs to get checked for an allergic reaction to the medication—perpetual goosebumps, eczema, lost hair. I go to the lab, joke with the nurse as she fills up tube after tube with my blood. I go upstairs and stare hard into a retinal scanner, a tonometer, a corneal loupe, a retinoscope. I get numbing drops, dilation drops, a poke in the eye, I go home.

I never imagined my mid-thirties looking like this: a regular schedule of attending to my health, always thinking about it, talking about it. I don't know true sickness, but I can say extended unwellness is awful, I don't wish it on anyone. But it's also an education in the body; I've never known this frame I live in so well. I listen, rapt, to the trials of my friends with celiac, with Lyme, with multiple sclerosis, with little-known autoimmune disorders, with unexplained symptoms that plague their lives. We trade stories. We're in our twenties, thirties, early forties, but we sound decades older. We say it to each other again and again: *the body.* This subject I used to never think about—or at least tried to never think about—but now consider the most essential subject of all. The shell that unites all humanity but is so often used as an excuse to judge, to discriminate, to keep people separate, apart, alone. The terrain of so many dueling kingdoms: wellness and sickness, self-confidence and self-deprecation, love and hate, pleasure and pain.

[CODA]

END MATTER

A CATALOG

1.

IN TIME, MY RELATIONSHIP with my eye doctor changes—our battles morph into some form of mutual respect, or at least understanding. After a few more hemorrhages, each of which extends the existing permanent damage, I get on a loose four-to-six-week injection schedule. I surpass fifty injections and then lose count. I get clumsier, knock things over more often, miss details in my periphery. I become more light sensitive; it gets harder to drive on the highway at night. I think about when my grandpa stopped driving at night, a dozen years ago—when he was in his eighties, not his thirties. As my gratitude for my vision deepens, my trust in medical science warily does too. And, at the same time, my relationship to vision loss changes. The fearful reactions I had early on, ones I first put to the page over a decade ago now, seem exaggerated, uninformed, caught up in a past era of blindness limitations, full of misunderstandings, poor representations.

A pandemic begins and my injections for PXE and infusions for Crohn's are considered essential medical procedures, and on a couple occasions I'm the only patient in either department. With all of us double-masked, surprisingly calm, I feel like I'm breaking the rules, out in the world when I'm supposed to be at home, letting someone put immunosuppressants into my body when I should be boosting my immune system.

I get an apartment with my partner and her dog, both of whom have stomach conditions. We adopt an elderly cat with an elderly stomach. A dozen times a day we discuss our guts, but most days my vision is a bodily force that just *is*, a nonsubject. On other days, though, the quirks and errors of my sight announce themselves loudly, impossible to ignore. In this way, my vision reminds me that it will change and keep changing in ways I can't predict, something I've always known but have only started to accept.

2.

During the pandemic's first year, a small army of Helen Keller conspiracists amasses on social media—an assortment of people who believe, in various ways, that Helen Keller's story is not true. Some claim Keller fabricated the story, some believe her lifelong teacher and collaborator Anne Sullivan was controlling her and using her as a puppet, and some suspect Keller was simply not a real person at all.

Though some clearly don't believe the misinformation they're spreading and are just in it to joke around, to get a reaction, to troll, as I watch the videos I write down quotes: "She's a liar," "Twelve books isn't a reasonable number of books to write," "She's an experiment to try to motivate people that they can do whatever they set their mind to." Dozens of other lines sear into my brain but are too awful to put to paper. Watching it all—many of the videos mean-spirited or even rage-filled, all lacking any evidence to support their beliefs—I can't help but wonder if we've truly entered a new dark age, a time without nuance, without empathy. "The keenness of our vision depends not on how much we can see, but on how much we feel," I want to tell them, quoting Keller.

Then I think of another quote, maybe my favorite, from *The World I Live In*, Keller's stunning 1908 book about the intelligence of touch: "It is not for me to say whether we see best with the hand or the eye," she writes. "I only know that the world I see with my fingers is alive, ruddy, and satisfying. Touch brings the blind many sweet certainties which our more fortunate fellows miss, because their sense of touch is uncultivated. When they look at things, they put their hands in their pockets."

3.

One day, a different doctor does my injection. He's careful, slower, more interested in my history. "I'm just a little more hands-on," he says, and I hear the subtle dig—I can tell that he knows my regular doctor doesn't take his time, isn't hands-on. I tell him it reminds me of when I first started getting the injections, fourteen years ago, when doctors treated it more like a surgery. We talk about the larger gauge of needle they used back then, how common the procedure has become, and he says, "The things we can get used to." Then he pauses. "All these years later, and we're still just giving injections," he eventually says, shaking his head.

"What else is there?" I ask.

"The holy grail is of course a cure," he says, but he tells me about how a port delivery system is the likely next step. He tells me about new drugs, what the journals are saying, all the things I might experience or ask to try in the years to come. Then he gives the injection, washes my eye out repeatedly, twenty times over, saying, "I'm just very cautious of infections," and I leave with the biggest black floater I've ever experienced. I briefly consider switching doctors—the floaters come randomly, it seems, and his level of care and insight has me excited—but then the pain kicks in, the worst it's been in years, and the floater takes up residence. It stays for weeks, then months; it gets lighter but doesn't go away. Now it's a seemingly permanent fixture, bouncing around my field of vision, twinkling in certain lighting. Sometimes, when I go outside after being inside for a long period of time, it vibrates, like static on an old television, and each time this happens I remember falling asleep on the couch when I was a kid and waking up in the middle of the night, the world different, eerie, alien.

4.

Our dog looks at me with such need, even when my partner and I can't find a need that's unattended to. Some days it seems existential. As she barrels into her preteen years, aging suddenly in unexpected ways, it feels as if she's questioning life's purpose, or at least soberly considering how the various approaches to finding joy are all so fleeting. She's just fifteen pounds, a stilty Italian greyhound, but her personality takes up a room; she demands attention. She started staring more often during the first year of the pandemic, at first seemingly confused by the disordered routines, the elevated emotions. But now, a couple years later, it feels different, harder to make sense of. When we've already taken her outside, played on the floor with her, filled her food dish, freshened her water bowl, and still she stares, we lose our tempers. We're not proud of it, but something about the accusation of the stare—*you're not filling my obvious need*—gets into our anxieties around being good caretakers and we react out of the fear that we're failing her. Each time I lose my cool, I wonder if I still love staring. This isn't the fresh-eyed staring with a baby, nor the curious late-night staring my now partner and I conducted during the same time I was nannying.

Part of the staring could be that her vision is failing. We've noticed how she misses more and more visual cues and seems to rely more fully on her nose. I sometimes wonder if she's trying, in her own way, to make sense of the loss, the way she can't get our images in focus like she used to. Maybe the staring is just an attempt to see clearer.

On good days, though, I stare back. I look into the deep well of her eyes and we get lost in each other, finding meaning and connection there, it seems. I tell her she's good. "You're so good," I say, and she, in turn, in her own way, tells me the same thing.

ACKNOWLEDGMENTS

Michael Heald at Perfect Day put so much into this book. He really conceptualized what this could be and brought much-needed creativity and excitement into the process. I have so much gratitude for his work, kindness, and friendship.

Esa Grigsby copyedited the book with such deep care and attention. It was a dream.

Aaron Robert Miller designed the cover and was so wonderful and hands-on throughout the process. Each design concept he drafted could have easily been the cover, and I now like imagining those alternate-dimension versions of *Staring Contest*, sitting on bookshelves, looking far different than the one you currently hold in your hands.

Justin Hocking is the book's patron saint, providing guidance and sage-like wisdom at every stage of the process. He's possibly the most supportive person I know, and it's truly a gift to have him in my life.

Karleigh Frisbie Brogan and Margaret Henry read many of these essays in their earliest forms. Both gave invaluable guidance time and time again.

Michael McGregor got me to understand that this was a book, not just a few essays I felt insecure about. Without his insight, *Staring Contest* likely wouldn't exist.

Paul Collins assisted with a number of the research elements, including taking a strange and beautiful deep dive into the origins of eye-patched pirates.

Michele Glazer gave a close, poet's-eye look at an early draft of this manuscript.

Alexis Wolf and Ariel Birks read a number of these essays at various stages and regularly talked me through the writing process.

Christine Rutan gave an eleventh-hour read and caught so much that we had somehow missed.

The Acknowledgements, my wise and dear writing group, helped with many of these essays. Thanks to Lauren Hobson, M. L. Schepps, Tim Day, Katie Borak, Rachel Chenven Powers, Catherine Johnson, Nada Sewidan, and Molly E. Simas.

The Multnomah County Library, the Independent Publishing Resource Center, and the Portland State MFA program provided integral support toward the creation of this book.

Endless thanks to my family (all the Pacific Northwest Ambersons, Jeffersons, Uhls, Jussels, Horgdals, Andersons, and Mendozas).

Deep love to my friends and collaborators: Andrew Barton, Cole Cunningham, Chask'e Lindgren, Craven Rock, Gina Sarti, Kelsey Smith, Oliver Stafford, everyone from Sweet Babes over the years, and my lovely home-life family—Novie, Rosalie, and Sophie.

PUBLICATION NOTES

"Hazy" was originally published in *Catapult* (March 2019). Thanks to editor Matt Ortile, who did a lot of the cutting that got this initially very long piece to its more or less current length.

"The Eye Patch: A Brief History," "Staring into the Sun: A Brief History," "Bette Davis Eyes: A Brief History," "Poked in the Eye: A Brief History," and "A Machine for Writing: A Brief History," were originally published in *Hobart* as part of the "Adventures in Eyeballs" column and are currently archived on *HAD* (May 2019–March 2020). Thanks to editor Aaron Burch for taking a chance on this idea and always being so open and easy to work with. Series illustrator Betsy Agosta added so much to those original versions.

"Corrective" was originally published on *Vol. 1 Brooklyn* (January 2019). Thanks to editor Tobias Carroll.

"The Idea of Doing Nothing at All" was initially drafted for the *Alive in the Nineties* series. Thanks to series editor Aaron Gilbreath for helping me see that the piece wanted to go in a different direction.

"The Blind Cartoon" was originally published in *Columbia Journal Online* (April 2018). Thanks to editor Erica Stisser.

The title of the "One of the Styles of Living" series is borrowed from a commonly referenced line in the Jorge Luis Borges essay "Blindness": "Blindness has not been for me a total misfortune; it should not be seen in a pathetic way. It should be seen as a way of life: one of the styles of living." Many thanks to Leona, Keith, Andrew, and Sabine for offering their time and trusting me with their words.

"Captured" was originally published in *Propeller* (October 2019). Thanks to editors Emily Flouton and Dan DeWeese.

"Contact: A Catalog" was originally published in the *Stranged Writing: A Literary Taxonomy* anthology (October 2022). Thanks to editors Thea Prieto and Matthew Robinson.

"The Noblest of the Senses: A Catalog" was originally published in *The Gravity of the Thing* (October 2020) and edited by Thea Prieto and Matthew Robinson.

"Dry Eyes" was originally published in *Alien Magazine* (August 2020). Thanks to editors Claire Martin and Matthew Hawkins.

Elements of "A Machine for Writing: A Brief History" initially appeared in *Basic Paper Airplane #9: A Very Brief History of the Typewriter* (October 2015).

Elements of "Hazy" and "Off-Label" initially appeared in an essay entitled "Unsupported Transit" in the chapbook compilation *Dead in the Water* (Triceratops Press, 2015). Thanks to editors Sarah Tavis, Sarah Keliher, and Themba Lewis. Also, thanks to A. M. O'Malley and Hannah Horovitz for early suggestions on this piece, many of which guided me toward this collection.

SELECTED BIBLIOGRAPHY

For the sake of clarity and space, I didn't include most songs, feature-length nondocumentary films, television episodes, and personal interviews. A more comprehensive reference list can be found on my website: www.JoshuaJamesAmberson.com.

Hazy

Buñuel, Luis, and Salvador Dalí dirs. *Un Chien Andalou*. Les Grands Films Classiques: Editions Montparnasse, 1929.

Magic Eye: A New Way of Looking at the World. Kansas City: Andrews and McNeel, 1993.

The Eye Patch: A Brief History

Brooks, Charles Stephen. *Frightful Plays!*. New York: Harcourt, Brace & Co., 1922.

Holt, Ardern. *Gentlemen's Fancy Dress: How to Choose It.* London: Wyman & Sons, 1882.

Lester, Paul. "Slick Rick: 'You Learn from Prison Time—What Doesn't Kill You Makes You Stronger'." *The Guardian*, November 2016.

Mackay, Constance D'Arcy. *Costumes and Scenery for Amateurs: A Practical Working Handbook.* New York: Henry Holt, 1915.

Male Character Costumes: A Guide to Gentlemen's Costume Suitable for Fancy Dress Balls and Private Theatricals. London: Samuel Miller, 1884.

Nguyen, Hanh. "'Game of Thrones' to 'Twin Peaks': Here's Why Your Favorite Quirky Characters Wear Eyepatches." *IndieWire*, June 2017.

Ritchie, Anna Cora Mowatt. *Evelyn; or a Heart Unmasked: A Tale of Domestic Life, Volume 1.* Philadelphia: G. B. Zieber, 1845.

Schulz, Charles. *Security Is an Eye Patch.* Arlington, VA: U.S. Department of Health, Education, and Welfare, 1968.

Corrective

Brown, Michael J. "Is Justice Blind or Just Visually Impaired? The Effects of Eyeglasses on Mock Juror Decisions." *American Society of Trial Consultants* 23, no. 2, March 2011.

Corson, Richard. *Fashions in Eyeglasses: From the Fourteenth Century to the Present Day.* London: Peter Owen, 1967.

Drewry Jr., Richard D. "What Man Devised That He Might See," 1994.

Elman, Donald. "Physical Characteristics and the Perception of Masculine Traits." *The Journal of Social Psychology* 103, no. 1, 1977.

Goes, Frank Joseph. *The Eye in History*. New Delhi: Jaypee Brothers Medical, 2013.
Handley, Neil. "To Wear or Not to Wear: Changing the Social Norms with Regard to Eyewear." Public lecture presented at Gresham College, March 2012.
Marie, Jane host. "Mixed Signals." *DTR* (podcast) from Gimlet Media. December 2016.
McLannahan, Heather. *Visual Impairment: A Global View*. Oxford: Oxford University Press, 2008.
Paulus, Rick. "The Hidden Psychology of Wearing Glasses." *Pacific Standard*, January 2015.
Shields, David. *Remote: Reflections on Life in the Shadow of Celebrity*. New York: Alfred Knopf, 1996.
Whitbourne, Susan Krauss. "6 Messages Your Glasses May Be Sending People." *Psychology Today*, February 2016.

The Idea of Doing Nothing at All

Kopkind, Andrew. "Slacking toward Bethlehem." *Grand Street* 44, 1993.
Schuftan, Craig. *Entertain Us: The Rise and Fall of Alternative Rock in the Nineties*. Sydney: ABC Books, 2012.

Staring into the Sun: A Brief History

Bates, William H. *The Bates Method for Better Eyesight without Glasses*. New York: Henry Holt, 1943.
Huxley, Aldous. *The Art of Seeing*. New York: Harper & Row, 1942.
"Obituary of William H. Bates." *New York Times*, 1931.
Rawstron, J. A., C. D. Burley, M. J. Elder. "A Systematic Review of the Applicability and Efficacy of Eye Exercises."

Journal of Pediatric Ophthalmology & Strabismus 42, no. 2, 2005.

The Blind Cartoon

Maltin, Leonard. *Of Mice and Magic: A History of American Animated Cartoons.* New York: McGraw-Hill, 1980.

Maurer, Marc. "Of Mr. Magoo, Disney, and the National Federation of the Blind." NFB (archived) 1997.

Captured

Barthes, Roland. *Camera Lucida: Reflections on Photography.* New York: Hill and Wang, 1980.

Berger, John. *Ways of Seeing.* Penguin Books, 1972.

Butler, Heinz dir. *Henri Cartier-Bresson: The Impassioned Eye.* New York: NZZ Film, 2003.

Cartier-Bresson, Henri. *The Mind's Eye: Writings on Photography and Photographers.* New York: Aperture, 1999.

Dyer, Geoff. *The Ongoing Moment.* New York: Pantheon Books, 2005.

Evans, Walker. *American Photographs.* New York: Errata, 2008.

Frank, Robert. *The Americans.* Paris: Delpire, 1958.

Israel, Laura dir. *Don't Blink: Robert Frank.* Arte, 2017.

Maloof, John dir. *Finding Vivian Maier.* IFC Films, 2014.

Marshall, Colin. "Filmmaker Wim Wenders Explains How Mobile Phones Have Killed Photography." *Open Culture.* August 2018.

Sontag, Susan. *On Photography.* New York: Farrar, Straus and Giroux, 1977.

Trachtenberg, Alan ed. *Classic Essays on Photography.* New Haven, CT: Leete's Island Books, 1980.

Contact: A Catalog

Aron, A., E. Melinat, E. N. Aron, R. D. Vallone, and R. J. Bator. "The Experimental Generation of Interpersonal Closeness: A Procedure and Some Preliminary Findings." *Personality and Social Psychology Bulletin* 23, no. 4, 1997.

Bechtle, Mike. "Are You Talking to an Extrovert or an Introvert?"

Catron, Mandy Len. "To Fall in Love with Anyone, Do This." *New York Times*, January 2015.

Chiem, Richard. "Ten Times Gravity." *City Arts Magazine*, March 2018.

Ellsberg, Michael. *The Power of Eye Contact: Your Secret for Success in Business, Love, and Life*. New York: HarperCollins, 2010.

Faulkner, Michael Lawrence. *A Novice's Guide to Speaking in Public: 10 Steps to Help You Succeed in Your Next Presentation . . . without Years of Training!*. Old Tappan, NJ: Pearson Education, 2016.

Grace, Joanna. "Misconceptions about Autism: 3 Myths about Eye Contact with Autistic People." *Disability Horizons*, March 2022.

Hagen, Shelly, and David Givens. *The Everything Body Language Book: Succeed in Work, Love, and Life—All without Saying a Word!*. Cincinnati: F+W Media, 2011.

Jay, Martin. *Downcast Eyes: The Denigration of Vision in Twentieth-Century French Thought*. Berkeley: University of California Press, 1993.

Jones, Daniel. "The 36 Questions That Lead to Love." *New York Times*, January 2015.

Marcus, Ben. "The Dark Arts." *The New Yorker*, May 2013.

Rankine, Claudia. *Don't Let Me Be Lonely: An American Lyric.* Saint Paul, MN: Graywolf Press, 2004.

Robinson, Shelagh. "Eye for an Eye—Visual Violence." *Psychology Today*, July 2009.

Off-Label

"Avastin Treatment for Eye Disease." Macula Center. 2019.

Boyd, Kierstan. "What Is Macular Degeneration?." American Academy of Ophthalmology. February 2022.

"Cancer Treatment Controls Macular Edema Related to Diabetes and to Cataract Surgery." *Science Daily*. American Academy of Ophtalmology. July 2009.

Donegan, Lee-Ann. "Fears of Potentially Blinding Complication from Avastin Eye Injections Are Overblown, according to Penn Study." *Penn Today*. August 2015.

Finger, R. P., P. C. Issa, M. Ladewig, C. Götting, F. G. Holz, and H. P. N. Scholl. "Fundus Autofluorescence in Pseudoxanthoma Elasticum." *Retina* 29, no. 10, 2009.

Finger, R. P., P. C. Issa, S. Schmitz-Valckenberg, F. G. Holz, and H. N. Scholl. "Long-Term Effectiveness of Intravitreal Bevacizumab for Choroidal Neovascularization Secondary to Angioid Streaks in Pseudoxanthoma Elasticum." *Retina* 31, no. 7, 2011.

Mukamal, Reena. "Comparison of Anti-VEGF Treatments for Wet AMD." American Academy of Ophthalmology. February 2020.

Myung, J. S., P. Bhatnagar, R. F. Spaide, J. Klancnik, M. J. Cooney, L. A. Yannuzzi, and K. B. Freund. "Long-Term Outcomes of Intravitreal Antivascular Endothelial Growth Factor Therapy for the Management of Choroidal Neovascularization in Pseudoxanthoma Elasticum." *Retina* 30, no. 5, 2010.

Pollack, Andrew. "Genentech Offers Secret Rebates for Eye Drug." *New York Times*, November 2010.

Stone, Edwin M. "Can Further Studies Lower the Cost of Preserving Vision?." Howard Hughes Medical Institute. October 2006.

Tenenbaum, David. "Macular Degeneration Insight Identifies Promising Drugs to Prevent Vision Loss." University of Wisconsin-Madison News. July 2016.

Thomas, Katie and Rachel Abrams. "Paid to Promote Eye Drug, and Prescribing It Widely." *New York Times*, December 2014.

Bette Davis Eyes: A Brief History

Baldwin, James. *The Devil Finds Work: An Essay*. New York: The Dial Press, 1976.

Bianco, Marcie, Merryn Johns. "How Bette Davis Became a Hollywood Icon by Refusing to Conform at Every Turn." *Vanity Fair*, April 2016.

Canby, Vincent. "Film View: Bette Davis: The Epitome of Hollywood." *New York Times*, April 1989.

Davis, Bette. *The Lonely Life: An Autobiography*. New York: G. P. Putnam's Sons, 1962.

Dyer, Geoff. *The Ongoing Moment*. New York: Pantheon Books, 2005.

Hyman, B. D. *My Mother's Keeper*. New York: Morrow, 1985.

Shales, Tom. "Bette Davis." *Washington Post*, October 1989.

Sikov, Ed. *Dark Victory: The Life of Bette Davis*. New York: Henry Holt, 2007.

The Noblest of the Senses: A Catalog

Adamson, Peter host. "Eye of the Beholder: Theories of Vision." *The History of Philosophy* (podcast) from King's College London, 2013.

Jay, Martin. *Downcast Eyes: The Denigration of Vision in Twentieth-Century French Thought.* Berkeley: University of California Press, 1993.

Kleinberg-Levin, David Michael. *Modernity and the Hegemony of Vision.* Berkeley: University of California Press, 1993.

Kleinberg-Levin, David Michael. *The Opening of Vision: Nihilism and the Postmodern Situation.* New York: Routledge, 1988.

Marmor, Michael F., and James G. Ravin. *The Artist's Eyes: Vision and the History of Art.* New York: Abrams, 2009.

Mathieu, W. A. *The Listening Book: Discovering Your Own Music.* Boston: Shambhala, 1991.

Mathieu, W. A. *The Musical Life: Reflections on What It Is and How to Live It.* Boston: Shambhala, 1994.

Pallasmaa, Juhani. *The Eyes of the Skin: Architecture of the Senses.* London: Academy Editions, 1996.

Dry Eyes

Kottler, Jeffrey A. *The Language of Tears.* San Francisco: Jossey-Bass Publishers, 1996.

Lutz, Tom. *Crying: The Natural & Cultural History of Tears.* New York: W. W. Norton, 1999.

Trimble, Michael R. *Why Humans Like to Cry: Tragedy, Evolution, and the Brain.* Oxford: Oxford University Press, 2012.

Poked in the Eye: A Brief History

Bataille, Georges. *Story of the Eye*. Harmondsworth: Penguin Books, (1928) 1982.

Brothers Grimm. *Grimm's Fairy Tales*. 1812.

Buxton, Richard. *The Complete World of Greek Mythology*. London: Thames & Hudson, 2004.

Freud, Sigmund. "The Uncanny." *The Uncanny*. Penguin Books, 1973.

Hoffmann, E. T. A. "The Sandman" *The Best Tales of Hoffmann*. Dover Publication, 1967.

Meruane, Lina, and Megan McDowell. *Seeing Red*. Translated by Megan McDowell. Dallas: Deep Vellum Publishing, 2016.

Shakespeare, William. *King Lear*. Piraí: Floating Press, (1605) 2000.

Sitney, P. Adams. *Visionary Film: The American Avant-Garde*. New York: Oxford University Press, 1974.

Innervisions: A Brief History

George, Nelson. *Where Did Our Love Go? The Rise & Fall of the Motown Sound*. New York: St. Martin's Press, 1985.

Godin, M. Leona. "When People See Your Blindness as Superhuman, They Stop Seeing You as Human." *Catapult*, November 2018.

Leland, Andrew host. "The Secret Life of Plants." *The Organist* (podcast) from KCRW. September 2018.

Posner, Gerald L. *Motown: Music, Money, Sex, and Power*. New York: Random House, 2002.

Ribowsky, Mark. *Signed, Sealed, and Delivered: The Soulful Journey of Stevie Wonder*. Hoboken: John Wiley and Sons, 2010.

Staring Contest

Garland-Thomson, Rosemarie. *Staring: How We Look*. Oxford: Oxford University Press, 2009.
Stigh, Daniela, and Zoë Jackson. "Marina Abramović: The Artist Speaks." *Inside/Out*, June 2010.

A Machine for Writing: A Brief History

Adler, Michael H. *The Writing Machine: A History of the Typewriter*. London: Allen & Unwin, 1973.
Linhoff, Victor M. *The Typewriter: An Illustrated History*. Mineola, NY: Dover Publications, 2000.
Nichol, Doug, and John Benet. *California Typewriter*. Directed by Doug Nichol, American Buffalo, 2016.
Wallace, Carey. *The Blind Contessa's New Machine*. New York: Pamela Dorman Books/Viking, 2010.
Wershler-Henry, Darren S. *The Iron Whim: A Fragmented History of Typewriting*. Ithaca: Cornell University Press, 2007.

Kingdom of the Sick

Sontag, Susan. *Illness as Metaphor*. New York: Farrar, Straus and Giroux, 1978.

Joshua James Amberson is the author of the young adult novel *How to Forget Almost Everything* (Korza Books), a series of chapbooks with Two Plum Press, and the long-running *Basic Paper Airplane* zine series. He lives in Portland, Oregon where he runs the Antiquated Future online variety store and record label.